All rights reserved. No part of this book may be reproduced in any form by any means without prior written consent of the Publisher, except for brief quotes used in reviews.

Meet me at the Well
PUBLISHED BY:
Authentic Identity Coaching, LLC
P.O. Box 36131
Indianapolis, IN 46236

www. Authenticinstitute.com
(317) 710-9533

Please contact
Authentic Identity Coaching, LLC
For Quantity Discounts

© 2017 Timeko Whitaker
ISBN: 978-0-9863401-4-7
Library of Congress Number: 2017913555
Printed in the United States of America

Book Layout by nVision International
Cover Design by Jo Gilbert
Photography & Cover Layout by Xzibitz Potraits & Design
General Editing by Dee Dee Cooper

Meet me at the Well

TABLE OF CONTENTS

Forward
About The Managing Editor
Introduction

1) ...And God Laughed 12
    Sharon Reed

2) Life After, And They Lived *Happily* Ever After 28
    Essie Foster

3) Change of Heart 42
    Danelle Cottle

4) Spiritual Recalibration/God's Hand Was On My Life! 56
    Lewis & DeElla Hall

5) I Let God 72
    Raenay Judeika

6) Are You Even Supposed To Be Doing That?? 84
    Karon Lancaster

7) Filter Out The Noise And Listen 98
    Margie Lea

8) Mother and Daughter Spiritual Journey 112
    Carolyn & Emily Loftis

9) GOD, Man, and Words: Whom Do You Believe? 126
    Kimberly Morris

10) A Walk In Miracles 142
    Evelyn Oglesby

11) Believing 154
    Jackie Thomas-Miller

About The Authors 166

Meet me at the Well

FOREWORD

As a Certified Christian Life Coach, there's nothing more fulfilling than witnessing the authentic journey of those who strive to move past every block and barrier in order to pursue and embrace the call upon their lives. Daily, I encounter amazing people with untold stories just waiting to be revealed.

Each author in this book has moved past warfare and into worship, birthing the very chapters necessary to make this book a valuable treasure. Every purposeful chapter was strategically written and every testimony shared displays His glory. God's intentional use of Pastor Sharon to unite each individual for this project is evident. With His help, her past and present touched to form a path of possibilities for each author called to this book project.

With each author's "yes", God gently provided the strength and courage needed to walk through the unfamiliar process. Warfare came for most, but grace, peace and love overshadowed all.

My hope is each chapter and testimony will ignite something deep on the inside of you, giving you the strength you need to face every challenge and pursue every dream. I pray the words emanate from the pages to bring light to dark places eradicating even a shadow of doubt regarding your significance and value.

Timeko Whitaker "Coach T"

About The Managing Editor

For Timeko L. Whitaker, there is power in authenticity. She shares her life-changing philosophy with clients and audiences across the globe, empowering them to reach higher heights, embrace their core values and achieve goals with her presentations and workshops designed to inspire, motivate and teach.

As a trainer, speaker, coach, author, and retired US military veteran, she is equipped to develop and train worldwide leaders and individuals alike, challenging all to live an authentic life of purpose. She is a certified John Maxwell Team Member, Speaker, Trainer and Coach, Founder and CEO of Authentic Identity Coaching, LLC and a certified Human Behavior Consultant specializing in (DISC) profiles.

Timeko has dedicated her business to helping all discover the power of authenticity. The guiding concepts of her mission are leadership, devotion and servitude. Combining the keystones of military service, including Loyalty, Duty, Respect, Honor, Integrity, Selfless Service and Personal Courage with key John Maxwell training principles, she shares wisdom and practical, applicable steps for those seeking personal and professional growth.

Through her company, Authentic Identify Institute, Timeko certifies others to become coaches and human behavior consultants.

After retiring from the U.S. Army in 2008, Timeko joined her husband, Eric Whitaker, in 10 years of Pastoral service, serving God through serving others. She holds a Bachelor's degree in Human Resource Management and a Master's Degree in Theology.

Timeko is the managing editor of Hidden Identity and a contributing author of The Power of Mentorship with notable authors including Zig Ziglar, Brian Tracy and others. She has coached both men and women to achieve their goals of becoming first time authors. Under her leadership, her publishing company has published over 60 first time authors.

Timeko serves as television host on TBN's WCLJ-TV's "Joy In Our Town" where she interviews community leaders, businesses and organizations who are making a difference in our society.

Meet me at the Well

While her goal is to help everyone she encounters embrace their authenticity and significance, Timeko especially cherishes her role as wife to Eric and mother of two children; Daelin and Eyuana Whitaker.

Authentic Identity Coaching, LLC
P.O. Box 36131
Indianapolis, IN 46236
(317) 710-9533
authenticidentity@gmail.com
www.authenticinstitute.com
www.johnmaxwellgroup.com/timekowhitaker

Introduction

"For God, who said, 'Let light shine out of darkness,' made his light shine in our hearts to give us the light of the knowledge of God's glory displayed in the face of Christ. But we have this treasure in jars of clay to show that this all-surpassing power is from God and not from us."
2 Corinthians 4:7

The City of First has another first with God's Authors of Kokomo women's book collaboration! God has liberally adorned us with his grace. These amazing, diverse women sparkle and shine with the light of the Lord through their testimonies. Each transparent facet of this book shows a view of their own personal encounter at the well. God saw fit to connect us to complete a mosaic of his work called Meet Me At the Well.

The authors have chosen to use what was once a burden, a fear or an obstacle for God's glory. Each chapter is a glimpse of the incredible awesome God we serve and his unlimited grace. We pray you will be able to relate to their stories and it will encourage, inspire, and provoke you to continue your journey with God.

Meet me at the Well

We have all been challenged and inspired by Coach T, an amazing woman of God, and we thank her from the bottom of our hearts for her leadership and vision. May this bring God much Glory!

The woman then left her water pots and went into the city.

Sharon Reed

Sharon Reed

An advocate for God, community service and leadership, Sharon Reed began her entrepreneurial journey with Esther's Place Boutique in 2006. She is an alumna of Ivy Tech Community College and Indiana Wesleyan University with a Bachelor's Degree in Management. She is a Configuration Management II Certified Professional, a Six-Sigma Greenbelt, certified for leadership development and Facilitating for Excellence and Business Consulting. She is a Leadership Kokomo Alumna and past director of the program. Sharon was ordained in 1999 and served as Pastor of Men, Women and Children (MWC) Evangelistic Outreach until 2004. She is the founder of The Esther Anointing Ministry. Sharon was

Meet me at the Well

commissioned as a Stephen's Minister at St. Vincent Hospital Kokomo and completed the Stephen's Ministry Leaders Training to train others.

With the belief we continue to reinvent ourselves, after retirement from Delphi in 2007, Sharon fulfilled her dream and opened Esther's Place Boutique. This was an antidote for her passion for fashion!

Her assignment with Delphi and the Ministry presented opportunities to travel globally. She received the Outstanding Professional from Indiana Wesleyan University, Ivy Tech Community College Distinguished Alumni 2007 Award and Sisterhood Christian Service Award from Women of Wayman in 2007 and was nominated for the Elizabeth Foster Award. In 2015, she was featured on the cover of Heartland magazine, Women in Business Issue.

Sharon serves at the First Church Nazarene on the Pastoral Prayer Shield. She enjoys spending time with friends and most of all her children and grandchildren.

Sharon is available for ministry, workshops and leadership development and can be reached at sarc332@gmail.com. Call (765) 419-4140 if you have any questions.

Sharon Reed

...And God Laughed

This morning, facing what is before me, I came into my home with recent situations flashing in my mind. My focus shifted to my disciplined goal of sitting before the Lord each day for 10 minutes where I lay all things aside to hear Him. I try to restrain the crowd from coming with me, the thoughts, worries, and fears. Just before meeting Him, I remembered my daily prophetic word:

> "God is going to confirm to you that He has not forgotten your situation." #dailyprophetic

Immediately the crowd arose before me.
- My daughter's addiction
- The doctor bills from surgery
- Taxes are due
- My mother's care
- My grandsons
- My pending divorce
- Oh yes, the book project!

Meet me at the Well

Then I heard the most awesome sound. GOD LAUGHED. My immediate response was, "Oh, no he didn't!"

I remembered my conversations with my father who is now with the Lord. He would tell me about his so-called troubles and I would laugh. He would say, "That's not funny." My response to God's laugh was "that's not funny!" His sweet spirit then took me to my shoes and showed me where on the inside of them I had written with a red marker, "Luke 1:37 For with God nothing shall be impossible," as a reminder with every step.

When my father would laugh at my current crisis, I knew it was because he knew it was going to be alright. So, this is why my chapter is titled "And God Laughed."

> THEN I HEARD THE MOST AWESOME SOUND. GOD LAUGHED. MY IMMEDIATE RESPONSE WAS, "OH, NO HE DIDN'T!"

THE BEGINNING OF THE FIRST HALF-CENTURY ... MY NICKLE

"Before I formed you in the womb I knew you [and approved of you as My chosen instrument], And before you were born I consecrated you [to Myself as My own]; I have appointed you as a prophet to the nations." Jeremiah 1:5 (Amplified Bible)

Early arrival by two months, my first battle in life was coming into this world. My twin sister did not make it. I was told she

was the healthy one. Pulled out of the womb with forceps and the incubator as my new home, I came with issues!
- The loss of my womb sister.
- The separation from my parents until I was healthy enough to go home a few months later.
- My need for special milk.
- My insecurities, thumb sucking and hair pulling.

Yep, that was me.

Another separation occurred when I went to live with my aunt, my mother's sister, until I started school. I saw my family periodically during that time, but had the love and care of a doting aunt and her son.

My mother said I didn't talk until I was three, but it wasn't because I couldn't. When it came time for school, they tested me to see if I was able to comprehend an aptitude test. I have been told they were surprised I knew all the answers. I started school a little before my 5th birthday and graduated with several scholarships.

About six months before my 12th birthday, I watched the resurrection story. As tears streamed down my face, I began to understand what had happened to Jesus. I let my mother know, I wanted to "join the church." To my dismay, I couldn't

join until I was 12 and that was a long six months away, but the day finally came and I made my way to the altar. I was read into Mitchell Chapel A.M.E. church and sprinkled.

Life's twists and turns produced a marriage at 18, two daughters, five grandchildren, a divorce, a ministry ordination, a church, a career and a business of my own. Most of all a deep relationship with my Lord and Savior Jesus Christ was developed. Many signs, wonders and miracles along the way increased a great faith and my thirst for finding God in the crevices of life. When I have a trial, I ask God, "Okay, how is this going to bring you glory?"

A SPECIAL DAY

"For I know the plans and thoughts that I have for you,' says the Lord, 'plans for peace and well-being and not for disaster to give you a future and a hope." Jeremiah 29:11

On June 5th, 2006, the Lord spoke to me and said next year this time he would show me his favor. He did exactly that. I received several community recognition awards. I was recognized at the state level. This was not just in the natural but a spiritual effect. In November 2007, I retired from Delphi and started my retirement with a ministry trip to El Paso, Texas and Juarez, Mexico where I witnessed God healing a woman's leg right before my eyes. When I returned, I officially opened my boutique, Esther's Place. This is my dream I have had since my youth. I was reminded when I had an assignment in Paris, France in 2005. As I contemplated life, I remember

Sharon Reed

thinking how much God had done for me. He allowed me to travel to various countries for my company and personal travel to Mexico and Israel. God miraculously opened doors for me to see China, Singapore, Korea, Germany, France including stop overs in Japan, Holland, and many cities throughout the United States. Many of the places I visited several times over a seven-year period and was able to connect to ministries and minister.

Now that assignment was complete. How would God use this experience in the future? I got to the point where I felt I had been so blessed and accomplished so much more than I could think or imagine. I wondered if I was getting to the end of my life. After some days passed and pondering how I felt, I sat and said to the Lord, "God you have blessed me beyond measure. You have given more than I've desired in the first half-century plus. I am not going to make a bucket list, THIS IS YOUR NICKLE! I am available to you."

THE BEGINNING OF THE SECOND HALF-CENTURY ... GOD'S NICKLE!

No regrets to my decree, but life has been unpredictable and challenging. Shortly after the decree my life was shaken with the death of my little sister Sandy, who suddenly passed away the day after we all celebrated her only child's high school graduation. Her only son, Alex, left alone at 17 years old. I left Indiana and quickly returned to Virginia to take care of her affairs and son, along with my brother.

Meet me at the Well

I had always doted on Alex and told Sandy if anything ever happened to her, I would take care of him. Our words are powerful! Grief-stricken and heartbroken, I put my life and business on hold. Once Alex was off to college, I returned back to Indiana. Grief had taken its' toll. Learning I was diabetic while experiencing extreme weight loss. I felt I needed to be in a place where I could be ministered to and the Lord spoke to me through a customer to visit First Church of the Nazarene. I did and I stayed.

I worked the estate issues over the next five years. Alex graduated from college and now he has a beautiful wife Nadya and lives in San Antonio. He is fine young man. It has been a huge blessing and honor to have been entrusted to oversee him. He has taught me so many things about life. There wasn't a day that went by during those years that I did not have at least one transaction regarding Sandy. I gained friends who were friends of Sandy that I still connect with and enjoy!

God's nickle ... Life was settling down a little and I met a man. Up until this time, I had been single for 25 years. He moved to Indiana and a year later we married. The next year, I learned that my daughter had an addiction to alcohol. A year after I married I got a call to pick up my two grandsons. The words I spoke to God rushed up before me. The boys came to live with us.

Sharon Reed

A MONTH TO REMEMBER

On September 15th, on my way to a meeting, I slipped and fell. On September 29th, my oldest grandson was hit on the football field and tore his ACL. On September 30th, my other grandson broke his hand. Our house was full of pain. Everyone except my husband was sick. The decline was approaching.

The dichotomy of being a grandparent and trying to parent two boys who are broken too was overwhelming. The weight of the situation was unbelievable. Then my father died within a few months. Counseling for my husband and I, doctors for us. I couldn't understand what was going on. I prayed and cried. One morning while going before the Lord, I asked Him what is this I am feeling and immediately I was taken into an open vision. The Lord said, "Look!" I looked down and pulled my chest open and saw my heart with blood running down. I rationalized pretty quick this was not a good revelation no matter which way I saw it. Not too long after this, I received a text from my husband that was not intended for me, but to another woman. We sought pastoral counseling.

In retrospect, I was so overwhelmed with caring for others and my health was at stake. I try to carry what the Lord was intended to carry. Jesus said in Matthew 11:28-30, *"Come unto me, all ye that labour and are heavy laden, and I will give* you rest. Take my yoke upon you, and learn of me; for I am meek and lowly in heart: and ye shall find rest unto your souls. For my yoke is easy, and my burden is light." (King James Version)

God's Order .... A Teachable Moment:

During the time our marriage issues came to light, I received a letter asking me to pray about being a candidate for our church board. It was in my heart to do whatever I could in my ministry. Having been a pastor, I was well aware of protocol when we have issues in our lives that need to be addressed and are in leadership roles. But, when I received the letter stating that the consideration for the opportunity would no longer be possible because of my situation, I was devastated. This was something I totally agreed with, but that did not dull the pain of the seriousness of my situation. I realized my authentic love for the Lord and my desire to do His will. I am thankful for a ministry that will address these types of circumstances.

I had lost my peace and needed to get it back. No one could do it for me so I decided to go on a 40 day fast. Half-way through, I started to feel settled. This scripture came to me: I Peter 5:10 *"But the God of all grace, who hath called us unto his eternal glory by Christ Jesus, after that ye have suffered a*

while, make you perfect, stablish, strengthen, settle you." We received more counseling individually and together. After a final meeting, we separated.

THE HEART OF THE MATTER...

Grandma's hearts are different. One day, I moved toward embracing my situation. It wasn't a sacrifice, but an act of obedience. It was a submission to God's nickle. Once the embrace began, things started to be more peaceful. Embracing my trials has been life altering. As I embraced them, I felt the Lord embracing me. I like the word "embrace" because it means: a close affectionate and protective acceptance. Protecting the holy. The holy is what God has ordained to be. This means not pushing our challenges away or fighting against them. Quality time with God and praying in the spirit has blessed my soul and spirit.

Raising grandchildren is entertaining and difficult. Their technological advantage and intellect is well beyond when I was raising my daughters. Although approximately 47% of grandparents are raising grandchildren, various community sectors and society have not yet adapted to be inclusive of this family scenario. There is awkwardness in attending school events, soccer and football games, but I find a lot of company there with other grandparents and the relationships developed with my grandsons' friends and their parents is a blessing.

One day I was praying and talking to God about having bible studies with the boys. He reminded me of the wisdom he imparts through me and as I walk through my life of faith and trust, my example is the greatest teacher. One of my grandsons wants to go on a two-year assignment to Ecuador. The other one knows he has a prophetic calling and shared he had prayed for a lot of kids at his camp. For this season, God has given me a specific assignment. My nephew and grandsons are the sons I never had. I can't wait to see what the rest of God's nickle has for me. No matter what, I plan to embrace it.

> I OFTEN SAY THE PHRASE "IF YOU ARE GOING TO WORRY THEN DON'T PRAY, BUT IF YOU PRAY, THEN DON'T WORRY."

The second time around raising children has taught me the importance of praying over my children and pleading the blood of Jesus daily. When they get on the school bus they hear....'the blood of Jesus on you!' I finish it once they are gone praying over the bus, the school and the rest of my grandchildren and family. This is an easier way and creates less worry about the outcome. I often say the phrase "if you are going to worry then don't pray, but if you pray, then don't worry." Maturity in the Lord gives you new strategies for century old issues in raising children.

Some grandparents don't get to see their grandchildren for many reasons. Now I need to make the most of my time

with them. I am believing God will deliver my daughter from captivity.

Sharon Reed -Corbett

"Though they join forces, the wicked will not go unpunished; But the posterity (children, descendants) of the righteous will be delivered (rescued, released, escape)." Proverbs 11:21 (New King James Version)

I want the boys to be godly young men. Wisdom that comes with age is a gift. Wisdom of young people who have gone through difficult situations is also amazing and needs to be recognized and encouraged. Thinking of ways to handle situations from the spiritual rather than emotional is better. Sometimes people say being around young people makes you young. I don't know if I can go along with that, but it does make you more savvy with technology!

With the epidemic of drug use, more Grandchildren will need to be cared for by grandparents or other relatives. The Al-Anon organization has been added to my weekly schedule. The meeting has been a valuable resource for support from people who really understand. I found it is not fair to expect your family and friends who have not had this situation to be understanding. This group meeting is for those who have someone in their life who has an addiction. It helps us care for ourselves with the help of God. We pray the Serenity prayer at each meeting.

SERENITY PRAYER

*God,
grant me the serenity to accept the things I cannot change,*

Meet me at the Well

> *Courage to change the things I can,*
> *And wisdom to know the difference.*

(The second verse is not known as well, but very appropriate)

> *Living one day at a time,*
> *Enjoying one moment at a time,*
> *Accepting hardship as a pathway to peace,*
> *Taking, as Jesus did,*
> *This sinful world as it is,*
> *Not as I would have it,*
> *Trusting that You will make all things right,*
> *If I surrender to Your will,*
> *So that I may be reasonably happy in this life,*
> *And supremely happy with You forever in the next.*
> *Amen.*

"The woman then left her waterpot, and went her way into the city, and saith to the men, Come, see a man, which told me all things that ever I did: is not this the Christ?" John 4:28-29 (King James Version)

There it is... the great commission. She must have had moments back at the well where she relived her first and

perhaps only encounter with Jesus. During my pastoral ministry, I went into a lighting business and the owner looked at me and said, "Show that woman Amazing Grace!" Amazing grace has been liberally applied to my life. I imagine this is how she felt. We all have had a 'well' experience if we have been saved.

A few years ago, we had a women's conference at our church. The women's committee asked me to be the keynote speaker and pray about a theme. I prayed for a couple of weeks and heard nothing. One evening with one foot in the bed and the other on the floor, I heard 'TELL THEM... I SAID, MEET ME AT THE WELL!' We don't know how often the woman of Samaria went back to the well where she met Jesus to relive the moment of her salvation. God loves me so much. He wants me to come back to the place where we began our journey and keep the moment of salvation fresh. He will meet me daily if I will slow down. He is still saying, 'BELIEVE ME, WOMAN!'

"Believe me, woman, the time is coming when you Samaritans will worship the Father neither here at this mountain nor there in Jerusalem. You worship guessing in the dark; we Jews worship in the clear light of day. God's way of salvation is made available through the Jews. But the time is coming - it has, in fact, come - when what you're called will not matter and where you go to worship will not matter." John 4:21-23 (The Message Bible)

And God laughed.... because He is sure of my future and it is all good.

"And we know that in all things God works for the good of

those who love him, who[a] have been called according to his purpose." Romans 8:28 (New International Version)

Essie Foster

Essie is a Personal Chef and the owner operator of a catering company called Chef For The day. She is a graduate of Aii, The Art Institute of Indianapolis, where she earned a degree in Culinary Arts. She is a community activist. She sits on the board of directors of The Reverend Doctor Martin Luther King Junior Memorial Commission and holds the position of Vice Chair Person and Brick Committee Chair Person. She also is a member of the Human Rights Commission of Kokomo Indiana and holds the position of Vice Chair Person. She is married to Ed Foster and is the proud mother/step mother to Bryant, Dionysos, Kim, Naomi, Jennifer, Stephanie, Ed Junior, Michael Ed and Christina.

LIFE AFTER, AND THEY LIVED *Happily* EVER AFTER

My journey to the well…

When I was asked to be a part of this project, I had no idea what was expected of me. When I learned the topic, MEET ME AT THE WELL, I was more confused than ever. So, I went to my Bible and I began reading John 4:1-42. I was familiar with the story of Jesus' encounter with the woman at the well. At first, I felt no connection to the passage. I reread it repeatedly and each time I read it, I asked myself what impact does this story have on me and how did this change the course of my life.

I looked deeper into what Jesus was saying to the woman. *"Woman where is your husband?" She answered, "Sir I have no husband." Jesus replied, "You are correct because you have had 5 husbands." John 4:16-18 (New International Version)*

That's when it clicked for me and I could relate. I had found peace years ago because of the love of our Lord Jesus Christ, the love of my faith and the understanding of church doctrine.

HUSBAND NUMBER ONE

I was no different than most young girls who dreamed about the day that their Prince would show up and he would be everything that she thought he would be. Tall dark and handsome, someone that you can count on, a protector. A God-fearing man!

I was like every other young girl who wanted the good life. After all, I had good role models in my grandparents and their friends. Watching them was like watching a movie. My grandmother, whom most of the family called Madea, while I called her momma, doted on my grandfather who she called sugar. He returned the affection by treating her like a queen. The sun rose and set for them in each other.

This was my world, the way that I thought every relationship worked. Little did I know that there was another side of the coin. A side, even with my active imagination, that I could never have dreamed up.

I always looked forward to Saturdays because I could go to the dance at the church, that is after religious education classes. It was fun and we could mix and mingle with the boys in the parish. The Nuns kept a close eye out to make sure

that you weren't dancing too close or any other undesirable behavior on the dance floor or in the corner of the gym.
I was standing near the bleachers talking to my close friend Nancy with my back to the dance floor. She was acting strange but I didn't know why. I heard someone say, "Not dancing tonight?" I turned and there was Angelo. At first, I thought he was talking to someone else. After all, he was one of the most popular boys in religious education.

We didn't go to the same school. He was a track star at Central High and I went to Shawnee, two schools that were worlds apart. There he was, talking to me and I was so nervous. He stood there in his white suit and he looked like a young John Travolta in that movie, you know the one, Saturday Night Fever.

After the dance, he asked if I needed a ride home? I told him no thanks. Nancy thought it would be fun to be seen with him, so I said yes. He was driving a white Cadillac, surely it was his dads. I found out later it was a gift from his father. We continued to see each other throughout high school. Mom and Dad were not fans of his because they didn't know him or his family, but I was thrilled. He was so exciting.

The first red flag I should have heeded was the night he took me home to meet his family. They lived in a very nice home in an affluent part of town. His mother, father, grandparents and great grandparents lived in the same home. They seemed to be a close-knit family. He had four brothers and one sister.

Essie Foster

The evening started out nice. When we arrived, you could smell the aroma of the sauce for the pasta wafting from the kitchen.

His father was sitting in his recliner watching television quietly and payed no attention to what was going on in the home except when someone got in front of the television. Then he would say something in Italian and whatever was going on moved to another area in the house.

Angelo took me into the kitchen to meet his mother and his grandmother. They were polite but somewhat out of sorts, it felt like to me. Suddenly, his mother started yelling at his father; his father said nothing and he continued watching television. She walked towards the door between the kitchen and the family room with a wooden spoon in her hand as she waved it around and continued to speak in Italian. Everyone in the home continued with their activities as if nothing was happening, including Angelo.

His mother entered the family room and stood in front of the television. That was the only time his father responded to her. Angelo's mother stormed into the kitchen, took the pot of sauce and threw it. There was pasta and sauce everywhere. I was afraid; I had never seen anyone behave this way. The strange part of it was that only I reacted.

Angelo went to the refrigerator as if nothing had happened, got some mortadella, made a sandwich and offered me one, while spaghetti hung from the ceiling and walls without taking a second look. It was as if nothing happened.

After graduation, we were married. One evening we were invited to his cousins' home for dinner. Before we could leave for his cousins, his father wanted him to run an errand for him. Angelo was gone for hours before he returned home. It was so late I had changed clothes and was ready for bed. He entered the room and saw I was not dressed.

I had never seen him in this mood before. He demanded that I get up and get dressed. I refused. He grabbed me by the hair, drug me over to the closet and began to pull clothes off the hangers and throw them at me.

I refused to put them on. The next thing I knew he was on top of me pounding his fist in to my face. I was pinned to the bed struggling to get away. Finally, I could reach the lamp on the night stand. I hit him as hard as I could and it stunned him. He rolled off of me and stumbled to the bathroom. When he came out of the bathroom he said he would be back and I had better be ready.

Once he left I struggled to my feet. I tried to call my parents but he had ripped the phone out from the wall. I got dressed and went to the nearest phone booth. When I got there, I realized I had no money. I didn't know what I was going to do. At the curb, I saw a man unlocking his car. "Excuse me Sir." He looked up and I could see in his eyes that he was

Essie Foster

concerned. "Are you alright?" he asked cautiously. I stood there for what seemed like a lifetime before I could speak. It was so cold that night I could see my breath. I only had on a sweater and no shoes. Finally, I heard a teary voice say, "Please lend me some money so that I could call my dad. He will pay you back."

He was heaven-sent. He asked me for my parent's name and phone number and dialed it. I stood there half listening as he spoke to my parents. He ended the call and said that he would take me home, where I would be safe. We didn't speak on the ride to my parents, but he sang a song that said everything was going to be all right.

When I arrived home, Momma opened the door and Dad was just behind her. I fell in to momma's arms. My father thanked the man whom he called Mr. Hill. Dad offered him some money but Mr. Hill refused payment. Everything was quiet for a moment then he added, "I hope if something like this happens to my girl, someone will help." Dad said, "God bless you," and closed the door.

> "I HOPE IF SOMETHING LIKE THIS HAPPENS TO MY GIRL, SOMEONE WILL HELP."

Dad called Dr. Young, who came to the house, examined me, gave me a shot and I floated off to sleep. The next day I went to the bathroom and when I saw my face, I was hysterical. My face was swollen two sizes larger and both eyes were black. I could barely open them.

Dr. Young assured me that the baby was all right. Two weeks later when I could travel, I moved to Indiana with my mother Mary. I did as Jesus had instructed his disciples in Matthew, when they came to a city that didn't heed their teachings. I shook the dust of Angelo from my feet and never looked back.

I STILL HAVEN'T LEARNED MY LESSON... HUSBAND NUMBER TWO

I was no different than many young women who bought into the instant gratification and the Hollywood version of what life should be with a husband, a house with a picket fence, children, two cats and a dog. Nowhere in that version of life does it say stop, listen, and wait for the Lord to lead me to the path he had planned for me.

Now, after the last experience I had with relationships and my poor judge of character you would think that I would do just that - stop, listen, and wait on the Lord. At this point I needed someone, anyone, other than myself to make choices for me; but nooo ... I dove head first into the fire!

One hot summer evening I decided to take my son to visit my ex-roommate Terry. When I arrived, she had company; his name was Dan. He was 6-foot-tall with long dark curly hair. He had chiseled features and he had a hot motorcycle!! What else could a girl want?

Essie Foster

He asked me if I wanted to go for a ride and of course I said yes. The ride took a long time and I began to get nervous. After all, I was on the back of a motorcycle with a stranger in the middle of nowhere. He could be a mass murderer, for all I knew! After what seemed like forever we ended up in the country, at a trailer with people I didn't know. In the back of my mind I knew that this could turn out badly. Thank God it didn't.

We became engaged. After we were married Dan took a job at the pottery. There was a bar directly across the street from his job and he spent most of his time and money there. Dan had a tab there and on pay day it was his first stop; he paid off his tab and whatever was left he brought home, which wasn't much. At tax time, the money would be spent on his motorcycle, regardless of what the children or I needed.
I felt that I had not listened to my parents nor did I wait for God to send me a mate, so this was my cross to bear. I never talked to anyone about my plight. I got a job so that my children would not suffer from my mistakes of choosing the same person in different skin.

I knew that whatever was going wrong was more my fault than it was the people I had chosen for a mate. I thought that because of church doctrine I had to stay in the marriage. I went on retreat and that is where I learned from my priest that I had it all wrong. Yes, marriage is a sacred sacrament, but God gave us strict guidelines which told us exactly what a marriage is. Love thy spouse as you love yourself. Do not covet thy neighbor's wife.

It had been a busy day with the three children and I had finally gotten them bathed and settled down. Dan had come home late and in what I called, "a happy state" and went to bed. There was a loud knock on the door. I went downstairs to answer it because whoever it was, they had a since of urgency in the way they attacked the door.

When I opened the door, there stood the police. "Is this Dan -----'s home and is he here?" I said yes to both questions. "Mam, we would like to speak to him."

I went upstairs and shook him. "Dan the police are here, and they want to talk to you." He got up and went downstairs; I followed him. When we reached the door, the police said, "Mr. -----" and Dan said, "Yes." The police stopped in mid-sentence, looked at me, and then asked me to please go back upstairs. I was confused, but did as I was asked.

We lived in an older home. There was a steam furnace that heated the house. There were grates in the floor so that the heat would rise to the second floor. When we bought the home, we put in baseboard heaters in the rooms upstairs but we left the grates in, so you could hear what was going on downstairs.

The police told him that they had had a complaint from a

Essie Foster

Mr. Patterson who said that he had had a confrontation with Dan that evening on his property about his wife. Now Mrs. Patterson was a coworker of Dan's. I knew her and had even babysat for her. I considered her a friend. They warned him not to return to the property. I was devastated!

A few weeks earlier Dan's sister and her husband had made a comment about seeing Dan in the parking lot kissing a woman, but Dan denied it. I believed him because of my upbringing. I couldn't imagine anyone who was married, being with someone other than their spouse. I was crushed when the truth came out. My love for Dan died that night. I stayed with him because I thought I was bound to him by the laws of God.

> I HAD PRAYED FOR A GOD-FEARING MAN AND HAD NOT RECEIVED HIM BECAUSE I WAS DETERMINED TO MAKE THINGS HAPPEN IN MY TIME AND NOT GOD'S TIME.

I attended a "Christ Renews His Parrish" retreat. During a one on one with my priest, he explained God and the church's meaning of marriage under Gods' laws. I was released from my misunderstanding of marriage and brought to the realization what I had was not what God intended a marriage to be.

FINALLY, MY PRINCE HAS COME

After everything I had gone through, I decided that it would

Meet me at the Well

be a long time, if ever, that I entered a real relationship with anyone. I had prayed for a God-fearing man and had not received him because I was determined to make things happen in my time and not God's time. After all, didn't the Bible say, *"Knock and the door shall be open, seek and ye shell find, ask and it will be given unto you?" (Matthew 7:7-8)* I had asked; I sought, and I found, but what I found was not God sent because I forgot to tarry and wait for Gods answer. Mom always said, "He may not come when you want him but he is right on time," one of her favorite Bible verses.

I was not prepared for what was about to happen one rainy afternoon. There was a thunderstorm warning out so the little league baseball game was canceled. My dear friend Lenny had invited me to an IBE membership drive. There he was, a very handsome gentleman, sitting there with applications for new members. He and I began to talk. Time flew by so quickly that we forgot that I was at the table to fill out a membership card.

It became late and people were coming in to attend the event. I wasn't dressed for the occasion so I said that I was leaving and explained why. He suggested that I go home and change clothes and come back. I thought about it, then said that I lived quite a distance from the event. His reply was that I should go home, take as long as I needed and he would wait for my return. I agreed.

When I arrived home, I decided not to go. My friend Teresa,

Essie Foster

talked me in to returning. She said that I could miss my blessing and never know if I didn't go back. I heeded her counseling, got dressed and returned. By the time I arrived the event was over, but as he had promised, he was there waiting. We talked all night and we have been together ever since.

God had fulfilled his promise. I asked and I found. I sought and it was given. I knocked and the door was open, and on the other side of that door was the God-fearing man that my heart desired. This man honors me and protects me. He is the backbone of the family, someone I know that I can depend on.

He is my gift from God, because for the first time in this long journey I stopped, listened and knew that he is God and he knows what is best for me. Never in my wildest dreams would I have imagined the goodness of the Lord and the abundance of love he would pore over me. My cup runs over, and his name is ED.

Yes, I met him at the well and was released of my transgressions and forgiven my deepest regrets of not trusting in His word. I know that he will never fail me because the bible tells me so!

Meet me at the Well

Danelle Cottle

Danelle Cottle was born and raised in Kokomo, Indiana. She is the mother of one son, Chase, who is serving in the United States Air Force. He is married to Jennifer and they have a son, Landon. They are expecting another baby in February 2018. She also has a daughter, Courtland. She is a senior in high school. She is active in sports and volunteer work. Danelle is a devoted mother and grandmother. She coached baseball and softball for 10 years. She has worked in the medical field for 20 years. She is a business office specialist at Advanced Medical Imaging. She loves sports, helping others, spending time outdoors, reading, and decorating.

Danelle is the owner of Full of GRACE inspirational gifts. She hopes to one day serve on a missions trip and she is passionate for Christ. She wants to share her story so others will build their relationship with God and strengthen their families. Her favorite passage is, *"By God's grace and mighty power, I have been given the privilege of serving Him by spreading this Good News." (Ephesians 3:7, New Living Translation)*

Danelle Cottle

Change Of Heart

The room was dark. I laid there as tears wet my pillow. Those tears turned into sobbing. The sobbing became so uncontrollable that I found myself gasping for air. The pain is indescribable. It is a pain that others cannot begin to understand unless they have been through it themselves. It shakes you to the core. It shreds your heart into a million pieces. You start to wonder how you will ever get through it all. I wondered, how will I ever be able to gather all these tiny pieces of my heart and put them back together. Has this ever happened to you? Have you ever been faced with a situation so unbearable that you didn't know how you would survive it? It doesn't matter what it is. Whether it is depression, addiction, divorce, or death, there is hope for total healing. That healing doesn't come from professional counselors or the best medical team you can find. A broken spirit, a changed life, a family destroyed can only be fully healed by turning your life over to Jesus. Only God can heal the brokenness in our lives. All we have to do is ask! *"The Lord hears his people when they call to him for help. He rescues them from all their troubles. The Lord is close to the brokenhearted; he rescues those who's spirits are crushed." (Psalm 34:17-18)*

BROKEN HEART

We have been together for 26 years, my husband and me. Our divorce is now final. That is God's will for my marriage and I accept that. Divorce is a nasty nightmare. It is the worst pain you will ever go through because it affects every single aspect of your life. People don't understand the complexity of your pain. It is worse than death. Death usually

> THERE AREN'T JUST TWO SIDES TO EVERY STORY. THERE ARE THREE – MINE, HIS, AND GOD'S (THE TRUTH). EVERY FAILED MARRIAGE HAS ONE COMMON FACT; GOD IS NOT PRESENT.

gives you closure. Divorce does not. It is like a tornado that destroys everything in its path. It affects you, your kids, your parents, your extended family, and your friends FOREVER. I do not wish it on ANYONE! Did you read that closely? Your kids, no matter what age, will forever be affected. The relationship between my son and his dad has been badly damaged. Our daughter took her hurt and buried it deep within her. She became very distant and rebellious. Watching her transformation was more painful than the pain from the divorce. She is the sweetest, most giving girl I know. She is tenderhearted and kind. She loves the Lord. Because I

Danelle Cottle

was so wrapped up in my pain and healing, I lost site of the fact that our daughter was hurting also. That is why I have decided to share how I turned my pain into your purpose. There aren't just two sides to every story. There are three - mine, his, and God's (the truth). Every failed marriage has one common fact; God is not present. Now, with that being said, this is where I believe our marriage failed. God was not present in my marriage. That was evident in our actions towards each other. God is about love. *"Love is patient and kind. Love is not jealous or boastful or proud or rude. It does not demand its own way. It is not irritable, and it keeps no record of being wrong. It does not rejoice about injustice but rejoices whenever the truth wins out."* (1 Corinthians 13:4-6) I was not kind to my husband. I was jealous, rude, controlling, always on edge, and kept a mental note of every single time he hurt me. He also admits to being a terrible husband at best. The enemy has a plan for each of our lives. The thief's purpose is to steal and kill and destroy (John 10:10). I allowed Satan to do that. There is no greater pain than family pain. Satan knows that. That is why his assignment is to destroy marriages. The only way he can do that is if we allow him to. I allowed Satan to take control of my life and my family.

THE HARDENED HEART

We were the picture-perfect family outside of our home but inside we did everything we could to destroy each other. I can't even remember when that all started. My husband is a racecar driver. My kids and I traveled from track to track supporting him. Our entire lives revolved around racing. When the kids started playing sports, I stopped going to the races. I spent all my time with our kids. Racing was his job. It paid our bills. I took care of the kids and he "worked." That is when my marriage started to suffer. I thought I was supporting my husband by letting him live his dream. I put my kids before my husband. He traveled a lot and had lots of freedom. That freedom caused our hearts to harden over time. Sometimes people turn their backs on God's perfect plan for their lives. Sometimes one party makes choices that will forever change a trusting relationship. My husband made the horrible choice of having an affair. Feeling worthless, like a failure, unattractive, humiliated, and broken hearted are a few symptoms of being lied to and cheated on. It is verbal abuse, only in silent mode. It is something you carry with you forever. At the time, I was not sure I would ever get over having an unfaithful spouse. I learned how to put my blinders on and go on with life like it was just a bad dream. It was a bad dream that I could never fully wake up from. I wanted that weight lifted. I had to forgive him. I couldn't ignore God. He commands us to forgive just as He has forgiven us. It was the only thing that would start my healing process. We both dedicated our lives to Christ. Our marriage was the best it had ever been. We were blessed in so many ways. Life was good! I was happy. He was happy. Then it happened again. I got comfortable in the happiness and I honestly trusted him again. When I found out he had broken that trust again, my heart became stone, cold hard stone. I allowed his behavior to continue. Instead of turning to God and trusting in his plan I turned to the enemy. I let bitterness and anger take root in my heart until there was no room for anything else. My only goal was to make his life miserable. Unfortunately, I achieved that goal. I wanted him to feel pain like I was feeling. When it happened yet again, I asked him to leave. That was the first time I ever asked him to leave our home. Instead of fighting for his marriage and keeping his family together, he turned to this other woman instead. All I thought about was what kind of woman sleeps with someone else's husband? What kind of woman is OK with destroying someone's family? What kind of woman wants to hurt my innocent kids? The question I should've been asking is, what kind of a woman had I become? I am ashamed that I claimed to be a Christian woman at that time. Going to church on Sunday means nothing. It's what you do from Monday to Saturday that matters. I was doing nothing to grow my faith. Marriage is hard but when you add infidelity, it seems nearly impossible to work on. With God, it is possible!

THE TRANSFORMED HEART

The bottom had dropped out of my life. I was barely hanging on. I was so exhausted from all the emotions and I could not concentrate or focus. I was easily sidetracked. I was exhausted, tired, and weak. I became withdrawn from all my family and friends. I had no desire to see or talk to anyone. The grief was more than I could handle. Then I cried out, *"Be merciful to me, Lord, for I am in trouble; my eyes are tired from so much crying; I am completely worn out. I'm exhausted by sorrow, and weeping has shortened my life. I am weak from all of my troubles; even my bones are wasting away." Psalm 31: 9-10 (Good News Translation)* Not all of God's signs are pleasant. Some are very painful. If those signs get your attention they are worth it. He was sending me signs that it was time to slow down, be still, and work on myself while he worked on my behalf. There is power in the word of God. When I cried out to Him, things began to shift. I felt that shift! I made the choice to concentrate on growing my faith any way I could. I began to talk to God. I asked him, *"What do you want me to do? What is your will for my life?"* Then I said, *"I want your will to be done, Lord, not mine but yours." Matthew 26:39 (New Living Translation)* I pressed into God's word by reading my bible, watching sermons on YouTube, being around strong men and women of God, and lots and lots praying. That is how I developed a passion for spiritual warfare. I am a very competitive person. I realized I was in competition with the devil, not my husband. I am also very passionate about what I believe. I'm not a quitter and I don't give up easily. The enemy is very smart and he knew these traits in me. Daily he would try to break me down. During my separation, I went through a tornado, had severe plumbing issues, a broken washer; my garage door broke twice; I had my first car accident, followed by another one a month later; my electricity had been shut off; my grandson was diagnosed with epilepsy; people would message me to tell me what they saw and heard about my husband, and the list goes on and on. Every day it was something different. Not once during all of those trails did I say, "Why me God?" Instead, I spoke to Satan. I stood up to him. I took authority over my life. I would laugh and say, "Is that the best you got?" God blessed me through every obstacle the devil put in front of me. EVERY DAY get up and get dressed with the armor of God. If you don't get dressed with it, the devil will kick your butt! He is full of tricks and lies. With the whole armor, you stand against the tricks of the devil! Your problems are not with your husband, wife, kids, boyfriend, girlfriend, boss, coworkers, or family. It is not flesh and blood we are wrestling against! We are fighting spiritual entities that cannot be seen with our eyes. Don't be impressed by Satan's power. He is the ruler of darkness. He knows your weakness and throws it in your face. Temptations, challenges, issues, and problems are the devil unloading all his guns at you. God has already given you and I the ability to fight and win! We must listen to His teaching of how. *"Be strong in the Lord and in his mighty power. Put on all of God's armor so that you will be able to stand firm against all strategies of the devil. For we are not fighting against flesh and blood enemies, but against evil rulers and authorities of the unseen world, against mighty powers in the dark world, and against evil spirits in the heavenly places."* (Ephesians 6:10-13). Do you understand that? We are not fighting against flesh and blood. Satan is real! He is also a master manipulator and a liar. When you become grounded by the word of God, you will be able to see through all of the enemy's schemes. When troubles and pain hit you, don't get upset with God. That is the devil's intention. Instead, admit that you need God's help. Thank Him for never leaving you. The best way to work through pain is to go through it. Just as a storm won't last forever, neither will your pain. It is a process. I had to allow myself to grieve the loss I had suffered. I realized I could not begin the next season of my life without accepting the pain. With all painful situations, we must face them. If we don't, that pain and suffering will eventually resurface in our lives. Trials are things that happen to us. Those trials also happen for us. They are not a definition of who we are. Remember, God made each of us in His own image. I needed this brokenness. When we are broken, God is just breaking away the outer hardened shell full of selfishness, pride, bitterness, anger, and so on - all those things our flesh has been holding on to. I thought my heart had been broken into a million pieces. I know now that it was God breaking away the hardness that had formed around my heart. He knew His word needed to be rooted in my heart. Once His word is planted, water it. It will then take root and grow! Keeping it watered will fill you heart full of love, peace, and comfort.

> TRIALS ARE THINGS THAT HAPPEN TO US. THOSE TRIALS ALSO HAPPEN FOR US. THEY ARE NOT A DEFINITION OF WHO WE ARE. REMEMBER, GOD MADE EACH OF US IN HIS OWN IMAGE.

MENDED HEART

You are the only one responsible for your own happiness. Sometimes God doesn't change our situation so we can change our heart. God wrecks your plans when he sees they are about to wreck you. We think our prayers are not being answered when in fact God hears us and answers. He answers them in the way he sees fit for his plan for our life, not the plan we thought we had for our life. Seek the joy in the journey instead of misery in the mess. Our suffering doesn't compare to what comes from walking with the Lord. I decided I wanted the blessings God had waiting for my kids and me. As I look back over the year leading up to our separation, I now see all the things God was doing to prepare me for this journey. I did an excellent bible study on the book of Hosea. That study taught me about true forgiveness and unconditional love. I used what I learned in that study to humble myself. I saw my husband as the man God sees him to be during our separation. He placed people in my life that would become some of my closest friends. They became my prayer warriors. They went to battle for me when I didn't have the strength to do it myself. They encouraged me to keep fighting and never give up. Two of my dear friends, Evelyn and Raenay, invested a lot of time into growing my faith and never losing site of the big picture in all of this. Evelyn was my "Miss Clara" as she sent me daily texts, would call and pray with me, and prepare me for the attacks of the enemy. She was the game changer in the growth of my faith. Our God is bigger than any difficulty you will face. Turn off the TV; put your phone down; stop associating with negative people and focus on the word of God. It is your most powerful tool. Praise him through your process. Focus on God's love. A broken heart can become a blessed heart if we allow God to do the mending. You have to find the strength God has equipped you with to fight and never give up. We must realize that a divorce should only be for biblical reasons, not selfish reasons. Marriage isn't something meant to throw away. Do everything possible to make it work. I worked on reconciling to the end. I showed our kids that you don't get married with divorce as an option. I showed our kids that you never take the easy way out. I showed our kids what true forgiveness is. I showed our kids what it looks like to be a child of God. Because I did all of these things, I have a true peace in my heart that it was God's will for my marriage to end. My marriage may have ended but my new life is just beginning. I have wonderful parents. I have a brother that would do anything for me. I have amazing kids. I have a great daughter-in-law, the most beautiful grandson, and another grandbaby on the way. I have a supportive family and a great group of friends. I am so blessed. I have a change of heart for the Lord. I can't wait for what He has in store for me in the future! I will continue to drink from His well. *"Come close to God, and God will come close to you." James 4:8*

PRAYER

Heavenly Father, you know our strengths and you know our weaknesses. You know the desires of our heart. You also know who you desire for us to become. You place us right where we are in every situation only for us to work on us and better ourselves so that your light can shine through us and help others. Lord, we are all under attack by the enemy. I thank you for giving us your armor to stand up to him and win the battle. In the name of Jesus, I cancel any assignment the enemy has on my fellow brothers and sisters, especially against their families. Father I know the reason you hate divorce is because of the pain it causes. Thank you for the grace you give us to get through each day. Thank you for never leaving our side. Thank you for your unconditional love. Thank you for the hope and peace that comes from your word. I ask that you place a "Miss Clara" in the lives of each struggling woman. Father God, we expect you to do great things in our lives! We pray this to you in the name of Jesus, AMEN

Meet me at the Well

Lewis & DeElla Hall

Lewis and DeElla met at her home church, Faith Temple Church of God in Christ in East Chicago, Indiana. After a two-year courtship they got married, moved to Kokomo, Indiana and have been married for 46 years. They are the grateful parents of two beautiful daughters, Deljere and Sherna, and three beautiful grandchildren that also love the Lord. Lewis and DeElla were both raised by devoted parents that loved God and raised their children to do the same. This love and devotion to the Lord would be the bond that would hold them together when their marriage would be tested.

DeElla is involved in missionary efforts, both local and international. This desire to see people come to Christ has taken her to Belize, Jamaica, Guyana and Costa Rica. In addition, DeElla being led of the Lord, formed a ministry targeted to women called "Daughters of Destiny." Lewis is active in the musical ministry and has been a tool unto the Lord since the age of 13.

Their greatest joy is assisting couples in their journey for their destiny in God. This book allows them to continue doing the Lord's work of building His Kingdom using the hearts of couples as a foundation.

The Ministry of God is so fulfilling.

Lewis & DeElla Hall

SPIRITUAL RECALIBRATION
LEWIS HALL

"Therefore, since we are surrounded by such a great cloud of witnesses, let us throw off everything that hinders and the sin that so easily entangles. And let us run with perseverance the race marked out for us…" Hebrews 12:1-3 (King James Version)

When life presents us with opportunities, we look at the paths and determine which one will take us to an intended goal. The goal we are seeking we believe will satisfy our pursuit to the degree that we feel the journey was worthwhile and fulfilling. If not, we will then look and choose another path that we earnestly believe to be the one that will offer us the much sought-after joy and delight. The joy of the journey is often a precursor to what lies ahead and that joy keeps us ever moving forward toward that goal which lies often beyond our immediate horizon. What happens when during our goal pursuit distractions occur and we find ourselves spent and headed in a wrong direction due to a bad choice?

What keeps us moving forward? What gave us the energy to initially move from where we lived without our goals and toward the horizon? What did we base our decision upon, what factor or what belief? What problem were we seeking an answer to? What solution would we find to apply to our situation? Would it provide a temporary fix or a permanent fix? How long would the urges be abated or maybe even completely go away? There have been so many attempts to patch the hole in our existence that seemingly never was filled or attended to in the correct manner. There was a thirsting in the soul that needed satisfying. It is like having an empty cup that continuously needed to be refilled.

> GOD BEING FIRST IN YOUR LIFE BRINGS ORDER; CONVERSELY, GOD NOT BEING FIRST BRINGS DISORDER.

God being first in your life brings order; conversely, God not being first brings disorder. When your life's pursuit is godly all of your goal achievements, goal obtainments and all of the comforts and treasures you have received honor God. Experiencing godlessness in your efforts you will first encounter hindrances. These are the Holy Spirit's way of saying turn around, you are headed in the wrong direction. Very similar to the GPS in a vehicle that says "turn," it informs us we are going in the wrong direction and when you turn it says, "Recalibrating." Failure to heed the warning after many wrong turns, the GPS dutifully continues to provide correct information on how to correct our wrongness. But failure to correct hindrances in life will lead us into the sin as Hebrews 12:1 points out. The woman at the well experienced this reality of walking in the wrong direction and hearing about the Messiah, but had nothing in her life that would allow her to alter her lifestyle.

It is easy to become impatient with God providing our substance and allowing patience to do her perfecting work in us. When we cease to be servants of God, we become servants to self and seek to supply our needs according to our own personal ability and using what is at hand to resolve life's needs. This takes God away which disorders our life and soon ungodly things fill the vacuum and become important in our life's hierarchy of needs and pursuits. We find ourselves sinking and out of Holy Communion with God, no longer walking and talking with God as Adam and relating to Him in the garden. Disappointment and disconnectedness becomes our daily bread. Conducting our lives in bewilderment while continuing to make bad decision after bad decision, we soon realized the good choices were really bad choices disguised as good opportunities. We asked ourselves, "Will I ever get my destiny back? Can the promises of God be extended again, are they gone, forever?"

We spend our time with worthless pursuits chasing pipe dreams while the righteous sons and daughters of God enjoy his peace and fruitfulness. The enemies of our souls want us to waste our lives and time searching for that which do not fully fill. He laughs at us when he sits on our heart's throne because he loves destroying God's most treasured creation - you and me. We wonder how will I get out of this; where is the path to get out of this; where is the well that I might find the Messiah?

I remembered I did not have to go to the well to encounter my Messiah. I sought a minister and found one on DuPont Road in Fort Wayne, Indiana. A Lutheran pastor using the Hands of God picked me up and provided me with the gift of reconciliation. He told me how to recalibrate my life and prayed for me and on my way out of his office, I longed in my heart for him to pray for me once again. He stopped me before walking out and asked, "Can I pray for you once more?" My heart joyously melted while he prayed once again. On the way out he laughed and said, "Even us Lutherans sometimes get it right!"

Personally, I thank God for the many attempts by the Holy Spirit to re-order my priorities and place God first and the Grace of God that continued to be extended to me while in my state of disallowing God to order my steps. When I finally allowed Him to be reseated where I dethroned him, I found renewed joy, destiny and promises. I experienced newness in my marriage, my relationship with my children, my friends and my church. The woman went to Jacob's Well but thanks to our Savior Jesus Christ, the well has been relocated and it is now in our heart. Talk to Him and offer Him control of your heart and allow Him to abide in your heart and to become the center of your life. Give Christ the opportunity to sit at the top of your life's hierarchy of needs and desires. Let Him rule your well forever with His living water and you will never thirst again.

God's Hand Was On My Life!
DeElla Hall

"Before I formed thee in the belly I knew thee; and before thou camest forth out of the womb I sanctified thee, and I ordained thee a prophet unto the nations." Jeremiah 1:5 (Kings James Version)

I was the second born of 12 children. Our parents dedicated each one of us to the Lord. Our parents took us to church; the love of the Lord grew deep! I loved the church and attending; we participated in Sunday School, Purity, Youth Department, and Choir and traveled with the choir. I also traveled with my grandmother, Evangelist Pruvell Lowell, to revivals and prayer meetings. Prayer became a vital part of my life growing up. As a child, our foundation was solid and consistent. I really made the commitment to serve God when I said yes to the Lord in a revival in my senior year.

Jesus came that I might have life more abundantly. My

Lewis & DeElla Hall

desire was to please the Lord and marry a man of God. I was not going to yoke up with an unbeliever. I was taught this scripture, *"There is difference also between a wife and a virgin. The unmarried woman careth for the things of the Lord, that she may be holy both in body and in spirit: but she that is married careth for the things of the world, how she may please her husband." (1Corinthians 7:34)* So I waited; on purpose I delight myself in the Lord that he would give me the desires of my heart.

"He that finds a wife finds a good thing!" (Proverbs 18:22) I was single, saved and satisfied loving the Lord with all my heart. I was introduced to Lewis at my church in East Chicago. The young people were fellowshipping with us. He checked me out and we became friends. I didn't know at that time we would become husband and wife. We lived 2 hours apart. He courted me; it is nothing like it is today - long distance calling and writing letters. He visited me and stayed with our choir president and her husband, who were our mentors. When I visited Kokomo I would stay next door with his cousin.

We had fun and it was exciting. We were always attending church service. We fasted and prayed, witnessed to the unsaved; we desired the same things in life. We did everything to please God. Believe me the saints were watching and praying. They didn't believe in long engagements. LOL! He proposed to me in Ft. Wayne, IN in the spring during their District Meeting. And by July he placed a ring on my finger. Both churches, our family and friends gave us their blessing. God is good and we were married October 30, 1971.

Marriage is like salvation, you are going to have tests and trials!

These are the words God gently spoke to me one day, "Marriage is like salvation, and you're going to have test and trails." Wow! When you are so in love you don't think you would ever do or say anything to hurt each other. When we would look at each other and melt. It was that way before Adam disobeyed God! Those words coming from the Lord let me know there will be challenges. Our Aunt Dola testified one day and said, "marriage is not a bed of roses," and because we are not perfect people, we will have problems. This is all true; the word of God has every answer to our problems! Satan's job is to kill, steal and destroy.

> MARRIAGE IS LIKE SALVATION, YOU ARE GOING TO HAVE TESTS AND TRIALS!

There is no perfect marriage; we both have to recognize Satan's devices. We must fast & pray combating the devil. He is our enemy! There were a lot of couples in our congregation. One day I looked around and we all had issues, at one time or another. Divorce crept in the body of Christ. God spoke while I was leading testimony service and He said,

Lewis & DeElla Hall

"I hate divorce." In order to be on time for church sometimes the husband would leave the wife because she wasn't ready. She had to get herself and the children ready! Minor issue, right? But if Satan can destroy the families, he's destroyed the church. If we are arguing before we get to church, then our worship isn't pure. Marriage is wonderful. God ordained the institution of marriage. However, we all endure test and trails. Just as I made a vow to the Lord and promise not to take it back, we vow to love until deaths do us apart.

GODS PLAN AND PURPOSE FOR OUR LIFE!

We both confessed our calling and my husband was ordained Elder and received his license. I acknowledged the call to become a missionary and later became a licensed Evangelist. We had some trials along the journey! Yet I had the victory. The devil was mad. We desired a child for seven years and this was a trying time for both of us. There was disappointment every month. The enemy tried to bring a wedge between us. We were visiting church, coming down the stairs at Faith Church of God in Christ in Indianapolis and missionary Dillion's son Damon looked at me and said, "You are going to have two girls." After building our home in 1977, traveling some, God did as promised and blessed me to give birth to our 1st born daughter on Dec. 4, 1980. On September 15, 1982, God gave us another beautiful baby girl! God blessed me to stay home from work to take care of the girls for 10 years and then I went back to work. We were blessed. They brought joy and we gave them to the Lord and taught them to love the Lord. God knows the plans for our life, it's good! Jeremiah 29:11-12.

I was very involved in the church work, but God was calling me to a life of prayer and ministry. He had a great work for me. Elder Joel said, "God is calling you out of the 4 walls of Grace!" I received every word that was spoken. Then again, the same word was spoken to me. Another prophecy was spoken to me about a women's ministry. I said, "Your will Lord, not my will." Marriage, new home, children, great church, family, and a job - the American dream. Praise Him! There is nothing wrong with this. I started to seek God and ask Him, what is your purpose for my life? I need to know. One day during prayer two of the praise team members came to the altar. I began to cry out to GOD. There came up a deep, "YES LORD!" I said, "Yes, I'll do what you want me to do! Yes, I will go, yes, yes, yes!"

THE WARNING!

My favorite scripture *"Beloved, think it not strange concerning the fiery trial which is to try you, as though some strange thing happened unto you: But rejoice, inasmuch as ye are partakers of Christ's sufferings; that, when his glory shall be revealed, ye may be glad also with exceeding joy." 1st Peter 4: 12-13*

One Sunday during morning service, Elder Brown was being used by the Lord. He was praying for couples as God lead him. He said " sister Hall go to your husband " I went to the

Lewis & DeElla Hall

organ my husband was playing. Elder Brown placed my hand on top of my husband's hand and said, "You are going to go through something but you are going to come out all right!" I looked at my husband and said, "We need to pray." I was trying to figure out what was it that we were going to go through. We didn't choose this one; well we never get to pick and choose our test and trials. God gave that message to me during a home revival. I said, "If God had a list of sufferings, which one would you pick?" Guess what? No one would get up and choose from the list, because we don't want to go through anything! Wow!

Shortly after the word from the Lord, God told me to tell the Pastor, the late Bishop Hall, to re-establish the Monday night prayer. So I did, but I also told the pastor I knew the prayer was for me! I said to Bishop Hall that people can get delivered because of our mouths. Because of gossiping and cliques, we had become the lukewarm church! God said, "I'm coming through this house and separating the wheat from the tare." Not knowing he was going to call me up to tell the church what God said, so I shared with the church. Monday night, those that heeded to the call came out. God gave sister Beard the same message! Not only did we pray Monday night but God had us lying before Him interceding for the church and others Monday thru Friday.

Then came the storm in my home, our marriage, but God said if you take care of my business, I will take care of yours! It took a minute for me to stay focused when the trials and the problems came like a flood. God actually told me to study Job so I did on my breaks and lunch at work. God spoke again and said, "I'm going to use your marriage for Ministry!" Prayer kept me but I had to stay focused.

Calls were coming in from women at church and work asking me to pray for their marriage. They didn't know what I was going through. As a matter of fact, some didn't know me and they would literally walk up to me and download. I would say, "STOP, I know what to do!" I had to pray with them and teach them how to fight the enemy! I gave them scriptures to fight with, 2 Corinthians 10:4, Ephesian 6:12-13. I would drive out of town to meet them, pray, anoint, and encourage. One day I got my hands on the *Power of a Praying Wife* by Stormie Omartian, purchased over 40 copies and gave them out, and later gave men the *Power of a Praying Husband*.God healed the broken-hearted and restored marriages. Women would come by and my husband would know when they came, it was for prayer or the book. When the heat got hotter, the Holy ghost in me got on fire. I knew I had the victory because I told him I didn't know what he was going to do, but I had to do what God had for me!

God said, "This is not about you." Evangelist Stallworth coached me through this time of testing. We continued the evening prayer and it grew. People were seeking God and forgiving one another. At this point God had told me not to say a word to my husband. He came maybe twice but his heart wasn't there. In the prayer, Associate Pastor Beard and his

Lewis & DeElla Hall

wife Wanda didn't miss a beat. After months of praying, one night God released me to pray for my husband. God then instructed me to ask seven couples to pray for us and none of them asked questions! I believe they did just that - prayed. During this entire time, I would repeat Elder Browns's words, remember "he told us, 'you're going thru something but you are going to come out alright!" God did - He delivered my husband and brought restoration! The one question he asked was, "What kept you holding on?" I replied, "GOD SAID I'M GOING TO USE YOUR MARRIAGE FOR MINISTRY." Over the past twenty years we've ministered to and prayed for hundreds of couples, pastors and their wives, couples living together and not married. However, God said it was for the CHURCH. God did take care of my business. We will celebrate 46 years October 30, 2017. To God be the glory! I stood on God's word!

Meet me at the Well

Raenay Judeika

Simple
Child of God
Jesus Follower
Daughter
Wife
Mother
Salon Owner
Nail Technician

"Trust in the LORD with all your heart and lean not on your own understanding (Raenay); in all your ways submit to him,

and he will make your paths straight." (Proverbs 3:5-6, New International Version)

"The LORD watches over you (Raenay) — the LORD is your shade at your right hand; the sun will not harm you by day, nor the moon by night. The LORD will keep you from all harm (Raenay) — he will watch over your life; the LORD will watch over your coming and going both now and forevermore." (Psalm 121:5-8)

God doesn't need a bodyguard to protect you or a stand in. He himself is keeping watch over you. You are protected. He watches over your life. Today is not a surprise to Him. He's not scurrying around fretting over how He will get you through. You might be, but He's not. Let's thank Him in advance for handling our problems. Then whatever comes, know that He's taking care of it.

Raenay Judeika

$\mathscr{I}$ Let God

I

Hi. My name is Raenay Judeika and this is a little bit about my journey. I was born in Kokomo, IN and graduated in 1991 from Kokomo High School. I went to college for dental hygiene but couldn't pass my science classes so I dropped out and decided to go to beauty school to be a manicurist in 1995. At 23, I was now a nail tech. And I was good at it! I built a fantastic clientele and was making great money. However, I was single and didn't have medical insurance so I applied at Chrysler and was hired in 1999. In March of '99 I was full-time at Chrysler and quit doing nails all together. At Chrysler, I met my soon to be husband and we were married in 2002. I was 30 years old and we quickly started our family. Alec was born on May 6, 2003 and Brody was born August 3, 2004. And in 2007, I decided it was time to take the buyout Chrysler was offering and raise my kiddos myself.

I CHANGED

2007 was a year that brought a lot of change to my life. Bad & good. Some of the bad... I was home with two little boys all the time; I was depressed; my husband worked all the time. Some of the good... I was home with my two little boys all the time. I was blessed to be able to be home and raise them myself. In addition to that, I was blessed with a husband who provided for us. He worked a lot and I missed him but I also knew he worked very hard, long hours to support us. I decided I needed something more, something I had never tried before, something positive.

> I NEEDED GOD IN MY LIFE. I NEEDED HIM TO SHOW UP. I NEEDED TO FEEL HIM.

I needed God in my life. I needed Him to show up. I needed to feel Him. And it was my choice to seek him, not the other way around! I started taking my little boys to Church. They loved it and I loved this new comfort I had found. So that was my beginning. From that moment on I was all in with my growing faith and in February 2009 I chose to be baptized. I prayed about everything and still do! Prayerfully, in 2009 I also decided to start doing a few nail clients in my home. Since 1999 I had told myself I would "never" do nails again. For 10 years I never thought of going back to the industry that I loved at one time. But doing nails was always easy for me. Remember, I knew I was good at doing nails! So, I started doing some clients in my home. Most days I didn't get out of

Raenay Judeika

my pajamas. Ladies would come over and I would give them a great service but inside I was depressed and struggling to get out of that funk.

By now it is 2010 and I am 38 years old. My boys were both in school all day long. Still praying, I now heard from the Lord it was time to get out of the house during the day. I went back to the same little salon I had started in all those years ago. I built my clientele fast, doing the same type of acrylic nails that I did back in 1995. But now being a praying woman, I knew God had more for me. I was so hungry for something else. I just needed to figure out what the "something else" was.

I knew I was good at my job. I knew God had blessed me with this talent. It came naturally. But I also knew there was more to my industry then just doing artificial acrylic nails. So, I started listening to Nail Talk Radio. This is a station that airs every Sunday night. For 2 hours, all they talk about is nail industry stuff. I was hooked. I took in every word. One night in April of 2013, I learned of a pedicure school. I always enjoyed doing pedicures but really never had time to do them with all the artificial nails I was doing. In May of 2013 I went away for 4 days to Chicago and attended my level 1 class. I became Indiana's 2nd Certified Master Pedicurist. I came back on fire! I knew I had to drastically change how I had always ran my little business! I transitioned my clients out of acrylic nails to their natural nails with gel polish. I started telling everyone about my new passion to help care for geriatric, diabetic and problematic feet. I also started saying

Meet me at the Well

"someday I'm going to have my own salon" and "I know God is showing me what to do. I just have to be smart enough to listen!" I quickly started looking for a space to open my new salon. In August 2013, I had found it! In October 2013, I was open for business.

"I (Raenay) can do all this through him who gives me strength." (Philippians 4:13)

I LISTENED

God named my salon. I racked my brain for days, even weeks and no name was right. I, again, asked God to help with this task. I remember this night so well. It was definitely a vision in my dream. I woke from my sleep with the word "rethink." God answered my prayer loud and clear. And I knew that was it. The name made perfect sense. And so, Total Rethink was born.

TOTAL RETHINK Pedi Mani Care is the name of my new salon. So now I'm a new salon owner. And I am praying that God leads every step of the way. And he did and still is! Business is great and clients love the new space. They also love all of the knowledge that I am seeking/finding in the nail industry and in my faith!

In August 2014, I attended a life-changing event called the "Kokomo Great Banquet." I had wanted to go to this spirit filled 72 hours for a few years, but it just hadn't happened.

Raenay Judeika

This was the perfect time for me to be there. During the 72 hours I experienced The Father, Son and Holy Spirit like I had never experienced before. And now I was much better equipped for what was soon going to happen in my life. I know without a doubt the "Kokomo Great Banquet" grew my faith so much that when what looked like trouble came, I was able to praise God through it and thank Him for the work He was doing in my life. God is good all the time...all the time God is good!

I had soon outgrown my little space in which I had started. The 640 square-foot space was no longer big enough for the business God was conducting. So, I began praying for the next space. The building I was in had plenty of space to expand so I reached out to the owner and asked if he would be interested in helping me grow my business. I also sought wise counsel from a few Christian friends and they guided me how to pray. The Jabez prayer was one suggestion.

"Jabez (Raenay) cried out to the God of Israel, 'Oh, that you would bless me and enlarge my territory! Let your hand be with me, and keep me from harm so that I will be free from pain.' And God granted his request." (1 Chronicles 4:10)

I GREW

Oh, did that prayer ever work! And not how I thought it would happen. The night before I was to meet with the owner of the building to talk about expanding the salon, a quick heavy rain came through Kokomo. The rain fell so fast that it pooled on the roof and took it down. I walked into this mess the next morning, July 8th, 2016. It was definitely unexpected but I recognized right away that this was God's way, not My way and everything would be ok. We quickly moved everything we could to the other end of the building. This was a wide open huge space that looked like a warehouse. Not the higher end salon space I was anticipating. But it was a place to conduct business and I was thankful for that.

"For I know the plans I have for you (Raenay)," declares the LORD, "plans to prosper you and not to harm you, plans to give you hope and a future." (Jeremiah 29:11)

"So now what?" I thought to myself. So many people and voices telling me what I should do. And I could have totally taken control of this situation and made something happen. But instead I put my faith first. I know God is in control of this situation. So, myself and my employees made the best of the space we had to work with and we prayed. And I led my girls and my clients through this rough time. The surroundings were not what I had in my vision of what God had promised to me, but my faith was strong and I did not waiver.

I kept my salon in that space for the next seven months, July 2016 through January 2017. The space was dirty, cold, hot, wet and smelly. It was not at all what I had expected for my bigger expanded space. It wasn't remotely what I had in mind but it was bigger. And I was able to work in the space. I didn't lose any clients. If anything, I gained and built clientele for not only me but also my employees. That was a long time to wait to see what was going to happen. During this time, I of course prayed and listened to God. We had an old dry erase board on the wall that we made into our "blessing" wall. I wrote my desires on this board; employees wrote scripture and drew pictures and clients did too. It was a great visual to look at every day and remember the promises that God made to me. BE STILL! & THY WILL BE DONE! were the two promises I wrote on the board.

"He says, 'Be still, and know that I am God (Raenay); I will be exalted among the nations, I will be exalted in the earth.'"
Psalm 46:10

> BE STILL! & THY WILL BE DONE! WERE THE TWO PROMISES I WROTE ON THE BOARD.

I LOOKED

During those seven months, I looked and did my research on buildings to rent, lease or buy. I prayed before looking at spaces. First, I would always ask God for His Will to be done through me, for Him to use me. And then I would thank him for everything. I thanked him for the building I hadn't seen yet. I thanked him for letting me be able to go look at the space. And I praised him for being with me as I did the looking. I would ask God to be with me and guide my questions. I prayed for peace. I prayed for His will.

I looked at several spaces around Kokomo and nothing fit. Spaces were either too big or too small, too fancy or too run-down, too expensive or in the wrong part of town. No matter what the reason, I knew the answers I was getting were God's answers. This was my test from God. And I was not in any hurry to do it my way. I was doing it His way.

I KNEW

One day in January 2017 my phone rang. It was a man that had shown me other spaces that he owned over these last several months. He had a tenant who had just given him notice that his business was moving out at the end of the month. He said he thought this space might be perfect for me and wanted to know if I was interested in looking at it. Instantly I felt a sense of peace. It was easy. It felt good. I prayed for God's will again as I drove to see this space. It was perfect.

That is how God showed up in my business life. Once I decided He was welcome in my life, I had to prove to Him that I was serious. I strive every day to honor Him. In return, God answers my prayers in His perfect timing. In every situation that comes up I praise Him first. Whether it is good or bad I know my God has it under control and all He needs me to do is thank Him for it. Business life, and any realm of life, is so much easier letting God have control.

"See, I am doing a new thing! Now it springs up (Raenay); do you not perceive it? I am making a way in the wilderness and

Raenay Judeika

streams in the wasteland." Isaiah 43:19

I THRIVE

So, to wrap all this up, it doesn't matter where I have done nails. My house, someone else's salon, my first little cute salon, the warehouse salon or the nice big "I know God chose this" salon. God knew right where I needed to be and He has been right there with me no matter what the space looked like. He waited on me because He is a gentleman and never forces himself on anyone. He let me choose Him.

My story really is not about nails or pedicures or a new salon or old salon. It's about me finding my relationship with Jesus. It's about me choosing to start the relationship and trusting in God, then truly letting him have control and use me as He sees fit. It's about welcoming the powerful Holy Spirit into my body and letting the gifts of the Holy Spirit do its job.

My story is still unfolding. There are some great conversations that happen in the nail salon every day, several times a day. I am bold and confident when I talk about Jesus. I am intentional with decorations, music and retail items in my salon. I pray with employees and clients. I welcome the Holy Spirit to have His way.

The woman at the well and the nail salon are very similar. At one time, I was the woman at the well. And now I let my nail salon & gift shop be the well for others to come and meet Jesus. The woman was coming to literally get water. My clients are coming to literally get a manicure or pedicure. The woman got to talk to Jesus and hear how He knew her. My clients get to hear, through me, how Jesus knows them. And I know they can feel Him in my nail salon. They might not know what it is they feel, but they feel it. He lives in me and is welcomed in the space. And it is good.

"This, then, is how you should pray (Raenay): "'Our Father in heaven, hallowed be your name, your kingdom come, your will be done, on earth as it is in heaven. Give us today our daily bread. And forgive us our debts, as we also have forgiven our debtors. And lead us not into temptation, but deliver us from the evil for yours is the kingdom and the power and the glory forever. Amen'" Matthew 6:9-13

Karon Lancaster

In 2006, Karon suffered a life-changing injury to her back, severing and severely damaging nerves to her lower extremities. She credits the amazing power of God for her ability to walk, work and to take care of her family and serve her community in spite of what could have been a completely disabling injury. This life-changing moment is what pushed her to re-evaluate the way she spent her energy and her time. Karon is wife to husband, Greg Lancaster, step-mother and mother to their four children, Robert, Brianna, Paul and Ashlee. She attends church at Kokomo First Church of the Nazarene under Pastor David Leeder. Karon is a graduate of Ivy Tech Community College with degrees in Computer Information Systems (1998) and Secondary Education (2013). Having spent most of her years working in retail industries, Karon also spent 3 years with a tier two automotive supplier, and since 2010, has worked for FCA US, currently at the World Class Manufacturing Academy as a UAW Facilitator. She also serves in the community assisting with fundraising for the Kokomo Rev. Dr. Martin Luther King, Jr., Memorial and is an alumna of the Leadership Kokomo Leadership development program, class of 2013.

Should you desire to contact Karon, please submit an email to: karonlancaster@gmail.com.

Karon Lancaster

Are You Even Supposed To Be Doing That?

Focusing In On What God Would Have You Do

We are busy people. Busy with work, busy with kids, sports, church, friends, community, PTA- well, you know how the list goes on. And I was doing a lot of those things. I was taking kids to and from practices of sorts, helping with other people's functions, serving in different capacities at church, working 40+ hours per week on midnights, meeting with my kids' teachers and counselors, finishing my Associate's Degree in Secondary Education, serving my UAW Local. And I was tired. I was so tired. I was completely exhausted, physically, spiritually and emotionally drained. I was barely present in attendance at events. I was sleeping right alongside the girls track team between races! I was falling asleep on top of my homework in bed. And my poor husband and children were the suffering victims of my sleep deprived psychotic outbursts of rage and tears. But, hey, isn't that what it was all about? Being superwoman? Uhhh, no. As I was leaving home one afternoon, sans children, my husband called out, "Where are you going now??" I answered him with a quizzical look on my face and he said, "Why? I mean, don't you think you're doing too much?" I looked at him strangely and answered, "If God didn't want me to do it, He'd stop me." My husband shook his head and replied, "Did you even ask God? Are you even supposed to be doing that??" I had to go but his question remained with me. I thought about what he had asked for several weeks. I considered these questions:

How often did I cook anymore? It seemed as though it was days at a time between meals. And I enjoy cooking for my family. How many times did I yell at the kids? And why was I yelling so often? They didn't deserve that. I was transferring my stress to them and that was not their burden to carry. How much sleep was I getting? After all, the life of a night shifter is filled with constant disruption and the effects of sleep deprivation can be long lasting on the human brain. I needed to find a way to preserve my sleep. How do I really feel physically and emotionally? Could I even truly gage what was just exhaustion or pain anymore? Could I truly reflect on my emotional inventory through the brain fog I was suffering from lack of sleep? When was the last time I had a real conversation with my husband? Everything seemed to be just an exchange of information or some short "how are you?" If I needed his tenderness, had I "run him up on the roof" so-to-speak? And how much of my kids' lives was I missing? I was there, but not really. I was basically a piggy bank/chauffer

Karon Lancaster

for a few years. I wasn't participating in their lives, the way I needed to be.

Are you even supposed to be doing that? It rang in my ears like a bell in a tower. And so, I asked God, "Am I?" What would you have me to do? His response was, "What do you want to be doing?" So, I started to simplify. I asked myself a few simple questions:

> What is your assignment? Is this activity integral to the assignment that God has for me? Does it fit within the scope of my desires for my quality of life? Does it fit within the path for my altruistic and spiritual goals? How important is it? If I decided not to participate what are the direct and indirect consequences that will be faced by me or the persons impacted?

> Does it give God glory? Ultimately, this is the goal in my life. Does what I am doing show the world around me who God is in my life? Just because God is okay with something doesn't mean that it's what I am supposed to be doing.

> ARE YOU EVEN SUPPOSED TO BE DOING THAT? IT RANG IN MY EARS LIKE A BELL IN A TOWER.

When I asked myself these questions, I reflected on the years of activity before and after I suffered a life-changing back injury. I looked at my level of commitment to my family and my church, to my extended family, my job and myself. I realized that I had suffered and my family had suffered with me. My children, especially my oldest, had borne the brunt of the crushing weight of a major injury and having to help support a household as I suffered in pain and weakness. My daughter was deeply hurt by the tremendous expectations put upon her and I have only recently come to realize the skewed perceptions she formed during that time that put us on a difficult road thereafter. As I recovered, it was during this time that I saw just how much I was doing before the injury. I was amazed at how much time I had to spend with my family and cook for them. I realized that none of the other activities I thought I was so integral to, were continuing just fine without me. So, I had a fresh start in determining what I should be doing with myself.

I had to examine how I was spending my time, what I was discussing and planning with my husband for our family and future. Did all the business I had filled my life with actually serve a purpose in fulfilling the plans and future we wanted? Not really. I was not only fulfilling what I thought was important, but also helping support other people's "To Do" list as well! But in doing so, I was robbing myself of the time and energy I needed to pursue what God had for me. I was completely ignoring the fact that their goals had no relation to mine. Nor were their activities going to be able to support what I was desiring to do.

Let me first explain what my altruistic goals are in a nutshell. My desire, and I believe God's plan for me, is to serve my community. I want to see my local community truly come

Karon Lancaster

together, to become a "village" for our families and learn to respect one another's different walks of life, helping and teaching one another. I want a community where we respect and care for each other and our children especially, for they are the future community in which we will all live. I believe that God has equipped and empowered me to do so, and that my faith in Him is what propels and directs me in this challenging adventure. But let's be real – I'm doing it for myself. I'm selfish! I want a safe, beautiful community where children play together and families laugh together. I want to know that I won't have to worry too much about the poor in the community seeking desperate measures because the community takes care of the poor. I want to see a community where we nurture our children AS A VILLAGE and take the time to equip them with the skills and knowledge- and love- they need to be self-reliant, capable, and involved citizens in our community. I want to help cultivate leaders in our community who will lead our neighborhoods with a solid moral compass and govern our city with wisdom to consider both the visible and invisible members of our community. Basically, I wanna change the world, okay? But only for my own family's benefit and anyone else is a bonus. (note the wink here…)

I thought my assignment was to be a go-getter at my job and volunteer at the school all the time for the extra activities. I thought that attending every single invite, going to all the events would help me reach my goal. But that was wrong. I was just spinning my wheels. And when I herniated a disc in my L4-L5 vertebrae, I learned the hard way what was more important. God. Family. Then Community. It was time to re-evaluate my priorities.

WHAT IS YOUR ASSIGNMENT?

Doors often open and close, there's a changing of the guard. Look to God's will for you. Don't allow perceived "restlessness" to distract you from what God wants you to be doing.

I streamlined the things that pulled me away from home too much -including how many ways I was involved at church! Wait, what?? But I thought I was supposed to serve the church! But how was I serving my home? I was wearing too many hats and it was tiring me out from being able to do what was necessary at home. I wasn't at home; I was at church. I couldn't prep dinner at church. I couldn't help with homework at church and certainly couldn't get laundry folded at church! This may seem like an oxymoron to others, but to me it became quite simply necessary. I was no longer able to function at the same levels as before, so I had to prioritize. The activities I included in my life had to center around how I was serving God and serving family first. I pulled back on the number of activities I participated in so that I had the time and energy to manage my household. I felt guilty at first, but then I realized that serving my family as a wife and mother is in fact honoring God! How can I serve in the house of God, but not my own?

Karon Lancaster

I then looked at how I was participating in my children's lives and at what level. I chose to chase my children. I tried to make every game, meet and school function that I could reasonably go to without impacting what we took care of at home. Surprisingly, it was a lot! I was even able to travel with the high school track team out of state and see college campuses with my daughter and create memories as well. And the reward was the smile on my children's faces when I was cheering, yelling at a referee or videoing a race. We worked as a team to get things done at home so that we could be free to do what we liked. Oh, and my husband loved seeing me leave the house for the cause of our children rather than someone else, which is its own reward! Oh, my heart was happy and overcame the guilt I felt about saying no to other commitments.

I also reconsidered what I chose to do in the community. I may not be able to volunteer in public events, but I can donate money, supplies or promote the cause. I began to consider my participation in an event to its relevance to my own goals. In order for me to dedicate my time and energy, the event had to meet certain criteria; does this push me toward my goals? If not, will this person's achievement make way for my goals in the future? Does my participation work against what I have set as my priorities?

At the end of the day, I must ensure that I am working in the right place at the right time and for the right cause according to God's will for my life. Anything outside of that can be a distraction that detours the path that God has set for me. I must rely on Him to direct my path and open the doors He wants me to walk through.

How Important Is It?

Wait. Pause. Allow time to think/God to speak. Does the longevity, time required/commitment create a result that ultimately meets your goals? GOD's goals for your life? If I decided not to participate, what are the direct and indirect consequences that will be faced by me or the persons impacted?

So often I would make snap decisions on committing to something without first considering the impact to my overall schedule or workload. If I saw an available slot on the calendar, I filled it. There was no consideration given to the level of importance of the request. I mean, picking up the flyers for the barbeque required an extra 45 minutes of my time, since it was 6 miles out of the way and I had to hand deliver them because the person who was originally slated to get them forgot and the meeting starts in an hour, never mind I'm supposed to be picking up the kids in 30 minutes, but the drop off is on the way.... Do you see where I'm going with this? It wasn't my responsibility, not my commitment, but I didn't just say NO. But I wasn't focusing on my personal or

> WAIT.
> PAUSE.
> ALLOW TIME TO THINK/GOD TO SPEAK

spiritual goals. I had to learn to stop and consider what the direct and indirect consequences that will be faced by me or the persons impacted. In this case, the impact to me was all negative: increased stress, more compressed schedule and none of it was related to what I needed to be doing now or in the future.

I had to learn to ask God what He wanted and then allow time for Him to speak to me. I now weigh the time required and longevity of commitment. And I pursue those commitments that are aligned with my own goals, God's goals for my life. I stopped feeding into what others were doing to pursue their own goals and started sowing seeds into others who were aligned with MY goals. Here I am daring to be a bit selfish again.

DOES IT GIVE GOD GLORY?

Is it pleasing to Him, what I'm doing? Is it part of his will? Can I measure myself according to the word with these actions? Does it lift my family up to him? Am I setting an example before my children in my walk with God? Ultimately, I want to please God in my existence on this earth. A few significant moments impacted my view on the world around me and I believe that God had me right where he wanted me to be to experience those things. I heard a song, a message, and saw someone treated poorly. The song "My Living is Not in Vain" taught me that even if I help just one person to know the right way, that is enough. Later, Reverend

Meet me at the Well

Elaine P. Walters, of the African Methodist Episcopal Church that I grew up in, preached a sermon called "I'm Looking For a Sister" that had a tremendous impact on me. She spoke of the need for us to stop looking down on one another as women and serve one another. She spoke of truly seeing the woman on the street begging for change, addicted to drugs or struggling to make ends meet. "I'm looking for a sister who is willing to serve!" Over 25 years later, those words still ring in my heart. Finally, I witnessed what would shape me for years to come and reminds me to be compassionate. As a young teenager, I saw a woman enter our church. She was poor, by the look of her attire, and was a larger woman, both very tall and fuller figured. She had several children with her - and she was white. As I watched her meekly looking for a place to sit without disturbing the service already in progress, I heard a woman from my church whisper (quite loudly,) "What she think she's doing here?? Coming in dressed all pitiful like that! And those children dragging in with her! What she think her black children means she should come here??" The woman heard her. She hung her head in shame and retreated to a rear seat, but left quickly after the service. I vowed that day that I would treat all people with the dignity and respect I want to be treated with. I realized what "church hurt" was that day. And I also learned that adults wear Sunday behavior along with their Sunday suit, so I'd better be authentic either way! These events, in addition to the stellar examples of service to others that were set before me by my parents and grandparents, all developed a desire to serve my community in a way that teaches dignity, love and creating opportunity.

Karon Lancaster

WHAT NOW?

Going forward, if I am to do what I believe God is leading me to fulfill in this community, I must maintain my focus on each of the goals he has for me. I must serve Him by serving in my family, my church and community. By serving my own family first, I prepare the way for my freedom to serve the church and community. I must set my house in order so that I can then easily and painlessly do what my heart desires. And I believe that God has put this desire in my heart. It burns deep within me to see our community pull together as a whole group, sharing with one another our lives and learning from each other. And I cannot do that unless I approach every opportunity presented strategically and spiritually to ensure it matches up with what God has given me to do. Is my living in vain? I should hope not.

PRAYER OF JABEZ FOR HIS BLESSING TO DO HIS WILL:

"And Jabez called on the God of Israel saying, "Oh, that You would bless me indeed, and enlarge my territory, that Your hand would be with me, and that You would keep me from evil, that I may not cause pain!" So God granted him what he requested." I Chronicles 4:10 (New King James Version)

PRAYER FOR GUIDANCE AND PERSEVERANCE:

"Show me, Lord, my life's end and the number of my days; let me know how fleeting my life is. You have made my days

Meet me at the Well

a mere handbreadth; the span of my years is as nothing before you. Everyone is but a breath, even those who seem secure…But now, Lord, what do I look for? My hope is in You."
Psalms 39:4-7 (New International Version)

Margie Lea

Margie Lea is the eldest of 7 children, wife to Sam for 35 years and mother of 3 daughters, one son and grandmother to 3 boys, all who are near and dear to her heart. She began coaching young athletes while still a youngster herself. Growing up in a large family gave her insight on teamwork and work ethic.

Although coaching was her passion, she felt the nudge to pursue a new adventure and followed her dreams for the next chapter of her life by becoming a Massage Therapist and building her own small business, "Margie's Sports and

Therapeutic Massage." She worked both careers for 15 years before retiring from coaching and focusing on her business and her family. Many children and adults have crossed her path and each one impacted her life beyond her wildest dreams.

Margie Lea

Filter Out The Noise And Listen

While sitting in the quiet room with soft music playing, I heard a strange ticking noise in the background. I listened more intently and heard the soft rhythm that it held and wondered where it was coming from. I followed the sound until I traced it to a small clock tucked in the corner of the room. The clock had been sitting there for over a year and I had not noticed its soft methodical ticking before. My mind wandered as I compared how the clock could represent God in my life and how many times he had been tucked in the corner and I did not hear him. I could hear the noise surrounding him but I did not always tune into his words of wisdom. God has provided a

> MY MIND WANDERED AS I COMPARED HOW THE CLOCK COULD REPRESENT GOD IN MY LIFE AND HOW MANY TIMES HE HAD BEEN TUCKED IN THE CORNER AND I DID NOT HEAR HIM.

well, filled with wisdom and knowledge for us to draw from, but we must be able to filter it through his eyes to find his truth and instruction for our life journey. My heart overflows with the inspiration poured into me from the people I have known and met throughout my life so far.

LISTEN TO YOUR PARENTS

As I stood in the waiting area of the auto repair shop, I noticed a car partially covered with a tarp sitting in the back of the garage. I recognized the shape of the hood as well as the front fender. When I asked about the car under the tarp, I learned that the mechanic had been restoring it for a friend in his spare time. Suddenly my mind filled with memories of my first automobile. I purchased my first car just before my 16th birthday. I paid $100 with the money I had saved from babysitting and working a summer job in the corn fields. You would have thought I had won the lottery when I sat behind the wheel of my very own slightly dented, somewhat faded, noticeably rusted 1968 yellow Ford Mustang complete with automatic transmission and white leather seats. There were a few engine and muffler problems to repair, along with the fact that it had alignment issues that caused me to go through more tires than I care to count. All imperfections aside, she was a beauty and she was mine and I didn't have to share her with anyone, especially my siblings. The first repair made to my Mustang was the muffler. My dad suggested I get a sporty muffler that made a terrific loud sound so that everyone knew I was in the area. How cool were my parents to let their

Margie Lea

daughter have a loud, rumbling sports car? I had not made the connection until I became a parent of a driving teenager that my parents had an ulterior motive and actually kept tabs on me by the sound of that mustang. They seemed to know where I was, how fast I was driving and what time I arrived. The next repair was to the timing chain in which my dad sat on a five-gallon bucket and delegated to me how to take things apart and clean the oil off each piece before we put it back together. I most certainly was not impressed with working on an engine of a car. It became clear to me just how much effort, care and money it required to own a vehicle, especially a 10-year-old clunker.

I am the oldest of seven children. I would be the first to drive, the first to date, the first to meet catastrophe head on and the first for my parents to learn from. I honestly do not know how in the world my parents ever survived the seven of us kids. God has surely had his hand on my life for as long as I can remember. I wonder if the Lord ever thought that he had his hands full when I asked for his guidance for my life and then I took him on a wild ride. I am certain that my parents prayed for the Lord to guide me as well, most certainly when they were about to witness a train wreck and all they could do was pull up a seat and watch the crash. There were many! I seemed to jump into the car, put it in reverse and take off without looking in the rearview mirror to see what might be behind me. I had to learn the hard way that hydroplaning on standing water was a reality, that icy intersections would send me sliding through the stop sign no matter how hard my foot was on the brake and bald tires would send me spinning around in a circle eventually landing me between a pole and a tree, with inches to spare on each side. My dad made sure I was proficient in changing a tire due to the alignment issues and believe me, I changed many. While heading to work one afternoon, I came upon a railroad track with only enough room for one car at a time to cross over. I suppose it was a race to beat me across the track for the oncoming truck and my lack of ability to judge distance caused me to slow down. As the oncoming truck sped up, I chose to slow down to the point that we were both approaching the narrow track at the same time. I became so frightened that I swerved to miss the speeding truck that apparently wanted to play a game of chicken and I found myself crossing the tracks without a hint of blacktop road underneath me. I sat for a minute and examined the situation and realized very quickly that I had a huge amount of explaining to do for my parents to comprehend this mess I was in. My car had just run over the tracks and cut all four tires and bent all four rims. I began to organize the story in my mind as I walked to a nearby house to call home. I dialed the number and the kind lady who let me borrow her phone watched in anticipation as to what I was going to say to my parents. Of course, it would be my dad who answered the call. Clearing my throat, I said, "Dad, I have a flat tire." He responded with his all familiar suggestions, "Girl, you know how to change it. Change it!" I looked at the lady and said, "Dad, I don't have enough spares." I saw a hint of a grin on her face as I heard a sound of surprise in the tone of my dad's voice while he questioned as to how many tires would I need.

Margie Lea

My slow answer came in a low tone, sort of under my breath, "uh...four."

LISTEN FOR TRUTH

I can laugh at that experience 40 years later; however, I believe that little Mustang and all the adventures I experienced with it set the tone for my life's journey. I learned the value of listening to people who had more experience than I had. When I listened to wise advice, I was rarely steered in the wrong direction. I discovered that if I would listen and watch people who had already experienced the hardships and the successes in life then I would help myself refrain from the consequences that would surely transpire, such as dents in the fenders of my hopes and flats on the tracks to my dreams and aspirations. Proverbs 23:23 says, *"Buy the truth and do not sell it – wisdom, instruction and insight as well."* (New International Version)

Truth, Wisdom, Instruction, Insight... These are powerful and very valuable tools to live your life by. As I reflected on my inexperience and youth, I realized that I had hydroplaned over all four of them. I skimmed the top of truth, wisdom, instruction and insight, never really hitting solid ground. I sailed across them believing I had everything in control until life started

> TRUTH, WISDOM, INSTRUCTION, INSIGHT... THESE ARE POWERFUL AND VERY VALUABLE TOOLS TO LIVE YOUR LIFE BY.

hitting me with everything it had. I learned the value of truth, wisdom, instruction and insight and how priceless they truly are when coaching became my first career choice.

Coaching became my passion even though I had very little experience. Just like my first year of driving I became focused and fearless. I thought I could conquer the world. Landing my first varsity coaching job in the sport of gymnastics at 19 years old, then the varsity volleyball position a year later was an honor and thrill, but a huge responsibility. My first coaching mentor would be my own high school principal. He reminded me of the fact that I was not much older than the girls I would be coaching and that it was my responsibility to be a role model in how I carried myself. I never forgot his words of wisdom and instruction and I kept them tucked away in my heart and mind.

Youth and inexperience seem to open the door for all kinds of suggestions, words of wisdom, truth and insight as well as words of criticism that can be destructive to the core. Learning to sort out the wise from the destructive, the truthful from the disgruntled and the insightful from self-absorbed was a difficult challenge. I dearly wanted to be liked, loved and accepted as a person as well as a coach. I did not want to disappoint anyone nor did I want to fail. Criticism can either help you or break you. I had a strong group of volleyball athletes who were winners in just about every sport they participated in. After they had all graduated, the team began a rebuilding period and we lost many games. I was very stressed indeed. I had many words of wisdom, insight, truthful correction and not so constructive criticism accumulating on top of me each day. I am so grateful for the countless people, parents and colleagues who supported me and gave me positive guidance. However, the words that stuck with me all these years were from an upset mother who had every right to be as discouraged as I was. She was protecting her child, her treasure, her most valuable possession. I looked up into the bleachers as she began descending toward me in a rage yelling at me the words I can still hear to this day, "You are not a coach!!! You only had good athletes to work with the past 3 years, you have no idea what you are doing." Those words pierced deep into my heart and into the very core of my being. My mind raced, spun around and slid in 100 different directions landing between humiliation, shame and defeat. After repeating those harsh words over in my mind, reflecting on them for several days and experiencing relentless painful and deeply hurt feelings, I concluded that she was correct. I had been given an opportunity to work with some of the most amazing athletes a young beginning coach could have encountered. I learned so much from them and I realized that I had done a lot of things wrong and a lot of things right. I knew I didn't have enough experience to coach them on my own so I searched out the best college coach I could find at the time and asked for help. I was not so arrogant that I thought I could coach them with my limited knowledge so I found someone older, wiser and more experienced than I and we all learned alongside each other. What I did wrong was that I focused on the strongest athletes and failed to prepare the next group to take their place and continue the legacy. It was after that encounter that I found a new focus and a purpose for my coaching aspirations. I decided that my purpose in coaching would be to help each child accomplish skills that would help them reach their own personal potential, no matter if they were very basic skills or the most advanced while helping them find within themselves the desire to learn. I knew that if I could help young athletes feel that they had accomplished even the smallest skill then quite possibly they could take the experience and use it in any other avenue, challenge or journey in their life. That moment changed my perspective on winning and losing. Of course, I loved to lead athletes to winning seasons and personal goals; however, I realized deep within me that the process, preparation and time spent at practice was most important. Team building, relationships, and pursuing the same goal while working hard and finding their hidden potential was the heart of being a part of a team.

God put people in my life to give me wise counsel and sometimes it wasn't comfortable. If I wanted to be the best I could be then I had to learn mental toughness. If I expected my athletes to take a fall on a new skill and get up and try again, then I should do the same when I found myself in the middle of tough times. Falling on a piece of gymnastics equipment can break your body. Failing and making mistakes in life can break your spirit. One of the best lessons we can learn during our training and preparation is becoming determined to get back up when we fall and try again. We need to become tough minded all the while learning from it and filtering out what is true and what is meant to give us correction and wisdom.   Humbleness and tough mindedness will inspire hard work, dedication and truthfulness about ourselves, all the while, developing us into the person God intends us to be. Proverbs 16:9 says, *"In their hearts humans plan their course, but the Lord establishes their steps."*

LISTEN FOR OPENING DOORS

Deciding to retire from coaching was a bittersweet decision. God had opened many doors for me and learning to walk through them wasn't always comfortable. I am sorry to say that I went through some of them kicking and screaming. God was so patient with me and when I listened, I experienced a peace in my decisions and going through the hardships helped me recognize the blessings.

My final gymnastics season would turn out to be dear to my heart. It was ironic that I would find myself in the same position I had been as a brand new inexperienced coach nearly 35 years earlier, rebuilding a team with very little chance of having a winning season. The athletes were hard working and dedicated but had not come together as a team after several months of team practices. Bonding as a team would be our greatest challenge. The team had many different personalities and levels of experience that don't always blend together easily. I knew we needed a breakthrough but I had tried just about everything I could come up with and it had not worked yet. Toward the end of practice one evening, I heard the girls coaching one of their teammates to attempt a tumbling pass. I was surprised to see that all the girls had gathered around to encourage her. She was a quiet and reserved girl who didn't always fit into the group as well as most of her teammates. I could see the excitement on her face and in her demeanor as she suddenly found herself fitting in. Finally, one of the girls called me over to give a little more assistance. I walked over to spot her on the tumbling pass but I did not say a word. I allowed her teammates to do all the coaching. She started down the floor, all the girls cheering her on but she failed to complete the pass. They encouraged her to try again, cheering for her and placing all their attention on her. She was their focus and she had a look of determination and confidence on her face that I had not seen before. She took off down the floor for the second try and this time she completed the tumbling pass. The entire team erupted and the smile on her face was priceless. As she ran back to the corner of the floor to try the pass again, I witnessed almost every single girl pull out their cell phones and begin to record her next pass so that she and her mother could see her accomplishment. I was stunned! At that very moment, we finally became a team. Several weeks later we had our first meet of the season which would be the last season of my coaching career. I told the girls that I had witnessed the very moment we bonded as a team and that I would never forget how they had encouraged one another. It was a moment in my coaching career that I would cherish forever.

Margie Lea

There was no logical explanation as to why that group of athletes could accomplish a winning season and advance to Regional as a team. They had pursued their full potential and reached it by working together and encouraging one another. Accomplishing our full potential is and always will be our greatest and most fulfilling adventure. When we are patient, things tend to work out just as they should.

At 16 years old, I began learning wisdom, instruction and insight from a slightly dented, somewhat faded, noticeably rusted 1968 Ford Mustang. I found that applying wisdom and growing in my faith would give me a stronger grip on the road of life which in turn would keep me from hydroplaning and sliding in circles around the person God intended me to be. I learned that being out of alignment with God would leave me discontented and repeating the same mistakes. I also learned that I can be restored with the guidance of Godly mentors and Godly wisdom that happens to be patiently ticking in the corner, waiting for me to filter out the noise of life and listen.

Meet me at the Well

Carolyn Loftis

Carolyn was born in India to missionary parents, Paul and Emily Cook. Both sets of grandparents were pioneer ministers.

She and her husband of 51 years, Charles, have three children and six grandsons. Carolyn attended Indiana and Purdue University for Tax Preparation and is an Enrolled Agent, qualified to practice before the IRS. She recently sold her business of 33 years, retaining the ministerial clients.

She attends Woodland Church of God, where she is active in teaching, worship, and many women's ministries. She recently received her ministerial ordination with the Church of God. She has been a speaker at women's conferences and events. She loves studying and being with family.

Her vision for the future is to be part of a Muslim Revival.

Emily Loftis

Emily is a freelance journalist in California, and therefore drives a taxi to help pay rent. She started writing at age 11 in a journal gifted from her grandmother, but has since picked up a master's degree at IU School of Journalism. She's written and fact-checked for publications including NPR, MotherJones, CaliforniaLawyer, Medium and Salon. Relevant to the book, she minored in Bible and Theology at Lee University.

Emily loves studying theology, collecting odd stories from taxi driving, experimenting in the kitchen, hiking with family, watching movie trailers with her husband and working on community projects.

Mother and Daughter Spiritual Journey

MAMA:

My dreams had been shattered. But when you confidently know the Word, the power of what and who God is, and your life shatters, you will survive. If He had not prepared me for the crisis in my life, I know I would have never been able to stand alone.

Emily was born nine months after the 1982 January blizzards. She came into my life while I was struggling emotionally. Immediately I knew she was gifted, reading at four years old and put into the gifted program at school. She was always asking questions. I thought I was giving her the correct answers, always from the Word.

At five she knelt by the bed of my Godly mother to pray. My mom shared later that while praying she became troubled.

God revealed to her a special calling on Emily's life. However, she would go through tribulations before yielding to her mission. I was somewhat concerned, but I knew that with God all things were possible. I would just pray and keep her in a Christian environment. She would be covered.

We went through many "Phases." She was a hippy child, one that challenged the norm. In her senior year she decided, after several ministers prophesied that she would be used in the mission field, she would become a professional potter. She would use the skill on the mission field to support herself and teach others. I challenged her to find her calling not just from her mind and heart, but from the Word. When God speaks to you from the Word and Satan tries to challenge your calling, you will have the Word to defend that calling. Her scripture was *"But now thus saith the Lord that created thee,…..fear not I have redeemed thee. I have called you by name: thou art mine."* Isaiah 43:1 (New King James Version)

She became a pacifist, joined the Mennonite church and engaged into peace and justice. She attended a Christian university, got married (against our will), and went to India for an internship with her new husband. For several years they attempted to return to India, but after an abusive marriage and other obstacles in their path, they parted ways.

She went to California pursuing a career in journalism after her new boyfriend moved there to help start a new business. She migrated from a pacifist to an activist with Occupy

Oakland, involved in organizing and labor advocacy. I felt she had become distracted and confused by politics and how to change the world. In the Occupy Oakland tent camps she was befriended by Muslim African Americans. She was drawn to them since their moral standards were the same as her own, not partying and drinking. She said they showed her a "better way." All the questions she had about the Christian faith now made sense with the revelations of Mohammed. She said she always had questions but was afraid to tell me. She didn't want to hurt me. She assured me she was closer to God than she had ever been, but I doubted.

When she finally made her total conversion to Islam, I cannot even begin to tell you my reaction. Take a cold dull knife and thrust it deep into your heart and twist. My feet went under me; I could not breathe. This cannot be true. This is the child I carried for nine months, prayed over, nursed, rocked, sang to about Jesus. I cried and cried until I had no tears left. I watched her friends fulfilling their lives for Christ and could not understand what I did wrong.

> I WENT TO THE WORD FOR ANSWERS. NOT JUST TO MAKE MYSELF WARM AND FUZZY, BUT ALSO TO SEE WHO GOD REALLY WAS AND THE PROMISES HE HAD GIVEN ME.

I went to the Word for answers. Not just to make myself warm and fuzzy, but also to see WHO God really was and the promises He had given me. I read He cannot lie because He is God. One day, I knew that I knew that I knew. Not because of emotion, but because I buried myself in the Word. He transformed my mind and my heart. God had a plan.

That next year, God took me on a spiritual journey. It had been a hard year, but Emily and I kept in communication. No matter what your child shares with you, whether it is an addiction, an alternate lifestyle, a foreign faith, keep the doors of communication open. You must love them with Christ's nonjudgmental unconditional love.

God started speaking to me about my own calling. I was struggling with my own faith, trying to make sense of it all. I began the tradition of sharing the thirty days of Ramadan with Emily, praying and fasting for the Muslims. I was invited to a four-day spiritual retreat where I sat at the feet of Jesus and let Him speak to me. God reminded me of the calling He placed on my life and the challenge of my mother to take her spiritual mantle. I dedicated the next few months to prayer in my Prayer Room and finally submitted to the Lord's call on my life. I pursued my ordination not knowing where it would take me.

Little did I know the spiritual journey I had just taken was to prepare me for my greatest trial. That fall Emily came home to visit her aging grandmother and shared with me she would be returning soon, with a friend. We were lying quietly on our couches in the night. I suddenly became aware why she was returning so soon. She was getting married! I sat up gasping in tears. "Is it your friend that you have been talking about so much?" I felt as if I would not be able to breathe ever again. I felt my dreams spiraling down an abyss. As I lay there for hours, crying out to Abba Father, I felt I had to have answers. I stumbled into the next room where I found the Word of God opened to a scripture for the day. *"Peace I leave with you: my peace I give you. I do not give to you as the world gives. Do not let your heart be troubled and do not be afraid."* John 14:27 I went back to my bed feeling the covering of the Holy Spirit. I prayed in my prayer language, felt Emily's hand on me as I prayed. She stayed until I was in a peaceful sleep.

She returned with her fiancé in a few weeks. When he would go to his room that had been anointed with oil and prayers, to pray toward the east, I would follow him and go to my Prayer Room just across the hall. He prayed and I prayed harder. One evening after he had spoken to Charles, Emily's dad, who shared with him the difficulties they would encounter, he sat down to talk to me. I told him that Emily had a special calling on her life from God. I warned him that now he was part of that calling and God would not allow him to be an obstacle. He would be converted or removed. He was respectful and smiled in response.

When they left Indiana, without our blessing, he thanked us for our kindness and love. He had been concerned how he would be received in our home. Gently, I explained to him that it was only because of Christ's love within us that allowed us to love him unconditionally.

My family responded in different ways. My oldest son felt it was another phase in her life. She would get over it one day. My oldest daughter felt hurt by her sister's denial of Christ. She was concerned her children would be affected by this choice. She kept them at a distance, not communicating with her sister for a while. My sisters shared they knew this was coming. They weren't surprised. They were appalled that she would turn her back on her heritage and deep faith in Christ.

Recently we went to a delayed wedding reception, called Walima, in Oakland for Emily and her new husband, meeting his family. I helped her prepare the feast for family and friends while my heart still broke. I attended a prayer service at the Mosque and as she prayed prostrate before Allah, I clutched my prayer cross and prayed fervently. I was deep into my prayers, my protection from the pain of watching her. I heard her speaking to me in whispers, "Mom, pray quietly in your head!" I kept praying, but quietly. Even though she was trying to keep me from not respecting the reading of the Quran, I was not going to let Satan silence this Pentecostal mama in spiritual warfare.

This story isn't over. I praise God every day that she will be part of the Muslim revival in this crazy world. God will take her gifts and leadership skills to change the world for Christ.

I still seek answers. But without adversity, we never grow. Without pain, we will never feel compassion. God is taking me where I feel unequipped to go, but I know He will never take me or Emily to a ministry that He doesn't first prepare us. Now we see through a glass darkly, but I know the victory is in the making.

EMILY:

"Do you have a mother?" the Prophet Muhammad (peace be upon him) asked a man who had come for permission to go to battle.
"Yes," the man replied.
"Stay with her because paradise lies beneath her feet."[1]

My mother has always been patient with my never-ending questions. The rights I owe to her as my mother and the unspeakable love I have for her compels me to minimize her pain as I remain committed first and foremost to God. I've followed my questions into a faith that, despite her kindness and love, she believes to be damming. I can feel her mother's panic as she watches me choose what she sees as a path towards death. This is deeply painful for me, but the rest of my decision to convert to Islam has been obvious and organic.

I grew up in a Christian home with loving, listening, studied parents and grandparents who gave me a thorough Biblical education exemplified by humble, sincere practice. Despite that, the more theology I learned, the more questions I had. The confused issues were endless: the muddled paradox of "monotheism equals a tripart godhead," the shady relationship of the Roman Empire to the Bible's canonization (and the preceding repression of dissenting, anti-imperialist Christian communities), original sin, a soteriology based on human sacrifice, flesh as evil, nationalism and faith as bedfellows and their relationship to slavery, colonization and other heinous historical unfoldings, and the orientalist positions towards Judaism vs Islam. The list went on.

(Note: I know Christianity has a complex history of social justice, resistance and resource-sharing mixed into its record of bloody wars, racism and prosperity preaching, but I don't have the space to flesh all that out here.)

I tried different theologians and apologists. I went to a Baptist high school, minored in theology at a Pentecostal university, sought out the counsel of elders and professors, courted Anabaptist and "non-denominational" denominations and prayed and prayed and prayed to the One God I knew I still believed in. There were times when I felt somewhat settled, or maybe compromising in my faith, but I would always be tortured with a sort of cognitive dissonance. It's true that I believed at one time, that missionary work could be a useful vehicle for social justice. But after a high school trip to India, I felt unsettled with the idea of going to a place I didn't understand, full of religions I was uneducated about, to push a faith I was unsure of myself.

I went to college, still feeling an unspoken pressure from my family's legacy. A really wonderful professor had some progressive ideas about international service work that made

Carolyn & Emily Loftis

mission work feel more palatable. I went to India again for a class trip, but felt even more unsettled. Over the years, it didn't feel right. I didn't have the political or theological analysis fully developed to articulate my discomfort, but I couldn't go through with the career choice in honesty. I switched to an English major and accepted a state of perpetual confusion about my spiritual path.

I knew I believed in God. I just knew little else. What I have always known at the bottom of my soul to be true is that God exists and God is one; God is good and just; all humans have agency and dignity and accountability; we are interdependent; we must act because we are accountable.

A series of events related to a boyfriend and my journalism work led me to the West Coast. I quickly got involved in activism. A large part of the activist culture I had fallen into--mostly transplants out-shouting a community with its own history of activism-- felt a little discomfiting. Partying, individualism and condescending attitudes towards Abrahamic religions made me gravitate towards the Muslim community, which has overlapped with freedom struggles in the Americas since Muslim slaves were first brought here.

I found the Muslim community embracing, emotionally and materially supportive, honest, upright and knowledgeable. The youth I interacted with were extremely educated, the women strong and honored, the men respectful, the elders valued and the children accountable. Of course, the community wasn't perfect, but there was a lot to be drawn to. The more I learned about Islamic theology, the more I found answers to the questions I wrestled with in Christian theology. I began attending talks, studying theology and reading the Quran. I found Islam to be way more similar to Christianity than it was different. However, the distinction between the two faiths was seminal: a theology of oneness (one God) that permeates all other areas of theology; an obligation to self-determination and self-defense; consistent spiritual discipline (i.e. praying five times a day, mandatory alms for the poor, regular fasting). My faith in Islam grew as I learned about the meticulous preservation of the Quran in its original text. The precise methodology of scriptural interpretation gave me confidence in the doctrines and teachings.

I had made an intellectual journey to the religion, but at the end of the day, religion is more than just reasoning. At the suggestion of an elder, I spent a month of Ramadan fasting and praying for clarity to what I knew to be the nameless but undivided true God who had always been in my life and had always been near when turned to. By the end of the month, I knew I was Muslim.

I was still nervous, mostly because I was afraid to hurt my parents. I knew it would cause upheaval in the family, would be a difficult path in the Islamophobic political climate and would, in general, make my life more difficult in some ways. So I kept praying and I began to have dreams of comfort. My mother once told me that you know when something is right because you receive an unmistakable peace in your heart when you think of doing that said thing. I felt it. I know it's just a feeling, but what is faith at the end of the day? It's a subjective certainty. I was certain.

The aftermath was difficult: a terrified immigrant uncle feared more attention from the state, a silently angry sister, a dismissive brother, a confrontational aunt, a depressed father and a crying, engaging, loving mother. It was hard. It wasn't hard because I felt unrest from my decision. It was hard because my decision hurt my family. I pleaded with them, "What should I do? Lie to you or lie to myself?"

> IT WAS HARD BECAUSE MY DECISION HURT MY FAMILY. I PLEADED WITH THEM, "WHAT SHOULD I DO? LIE TO YOU OR LIE TO MYSELF?"

Even though my life had changed, I wanted them to know that I was the same old Emily. While a lot of converts change their name to a Muslim one, I kept my name--given to me after my grandmothers-- to avoid more hurt. I spent hours trying to answer theological questions and correct misconceptions. I made an intention to call my mother twice a week instead of once every week or so. I waited and made myself available for family members giving me the silent treatment. I bit my tongue in the face of heated confrontations. (Okay, I may have had a little trouble with that one...but I got better at it.)

Ironically, due to the efforts of my mother and myself, we

grew closer. It started slowly and painfully. My deep love for her and my Islamic obligation was to respect her more than anyone in the whole world, to go the extra distance with unconditional patience. So we talked. And cried. And talked. And cried. I'm not sure if I cried more at my hurt from wrong assumptions and disrespect from other family members or from the pain of seeing my mother in pain as a consequence of my uncompromising honesty. I know she hasn't let go of hope for my return to Christianity. She will believe what she believes about my life and I will believe what I believe. I'm okay at leaving it with that and I want to avoid adding any weight to her already heavy burden. I also pray that my Mother will find truth in Islam, the beauty and the comfort of the faith and the path of Allah. We now talk openly about theology, comparing stories and sharing experiences. We are far more similar now than when I was in an agnostic state of confusion. She will never approve of my faith or even my marriage to a Muslim man. However, our love and respect for each other continues to grow. The love between a mother and daughter, in any faith, is undeniably sacred.

Endnote:
Biblical Scriptures: Isaiah 43:1 NKJV, John 14:1 NKJV
"Do you have a mother?" The narration (hadith) as recorded by Imam Ahmad bin Hanbal in his Musnad. As narrated in Sunan Al-Nasai, Book 25, 3106.

Kimberly Morris

Dr. Kimberly Morris is a licensed Clinical Psychologist who received her Bachelor's and Doctoral degrees from Indiana University Bloomington. She completed both her clinical internship and 2-year post-doctoral training at Western Psychiatric Institute and Clinic in Pittsburgh PA. She has worked in both inpatient and outpatient environments. She currently works in the outpatient clinic with adults who struggle with anxiety and depression using cognitive behavioral therapy. In addition to her clinical work, Dr. Morris is an adjunct faculty member in the Department of Psychology where she teaches online courses in General Psychology,

Lifespan Development, and Abnormal Psychology. She has won 2 Amicus Awards from the students for teaching. Dr. Morris is a professional speaker who has a Facebook page, Inspiration for Life. She is passionate about sharing her psychological knowledge on mood, happiness and resiliency, compassion fatigue, womens' health and transition, stress/coping, and role strain with large and small groups.

Kimberly Morris

God, Man and Words

Introduction

I read a little purple book that forever changed my life, my relationships with people, and eventually my relationship with CHRIST. In his book, The Five Love Languages, Dr. Gary Chapman explained that there are 5 different ways that people send and receive love. Before reading this book, I had no idea why I could be so greatly affected by what people said to me. Compliments raised me up and criticisms completely tore me down. I was living out the verse found in Proverbs 18:21 *"Death and life are in the power of the tongue" (English Standard Version)*. This book helped me to realize that my love language is Words of Affirmation, which means that I send and receive appreciation and admiration through verbal statements (Chapman, 1995).

Being so driven by words was not a bad thing because I was surrounded by people who spoke life into me. My parents were big encouragers. My mom would tell me, "You can do whatever you want to do." Teachers told me how smart I was. Friends liked me and told me so. These compliments and encouragements built me up and I felt accomplished and capable. Surrounded by positivity, I had accidentally replaced GOD's words about me with man's words and in doing so, I had given the ultimate power in my life to another human being. This shift had huge consequences for me once I had a different group of people surrounding me. Have you ever allowed another person to shape you and your future because you didn't know the difference between GOD's words and man's words? This can easily happen if we don't have a clear understanding of the difference between the two.

> I GAINED A NEW UNDERSTANDING OF THE POWER OF WORDS WHEN ENCOURAGEMENT, APPRECIATION, AND ADMIRATION WERE REPLACED BY CRUEL WORDS THAT CRUSHED MY SPIRIT.

I gained a new understanding of the power of words when encouragement, appreciation, and admiration were replaced by cruel words that crushed my spirit. I began to lose my way especially when people told me that I was incapable of achieving my goals. My opinion of myself changed when I was rejected. I felt hopeless when my pathway was blocked by a person saying "No." John 4 reminded me of this relationship between GOD, man, and words. John Chapter 4 shows us how difficult it can be for JESUS to save us when we have been shaped by earthly words instead of Heavenly words.

THE WOMAN AT THE WELL

In John 4: 7-9, we learn about the Samaritan woman, who has obviously been shaped by the words of man. A teacher has instilled in her the laws of that time (verse 9). Someone told her about the limits of her performance on the job (verse 11). She apparently had felt judged by others because of her life choices (verse 17). Man's words set the upper and lower limits of life for the Samaritan woman. So, when JESUS appears and asks for a relationship with her, she eloquently explains why this is not possible.

First, she says that she is from the wrong side of the tracks (verse 9). Then she uses logic to rule herself out (verse 11). Finally, she disqualifies herself by talking about her past life experiences (verse 17). Each time, she quotes man's words to JESUS and HE recites HIS words of life back to her. From this exchange, we learn how hard it is for the Samaritan woman to accept JESUS' new interpretation of her because she has swallowed the interpretation of human beings.
Have you ever struggled with a sense of worthiness like the Samaritan woman because of words spoken about you?
Have you ever told GOD to avoid you because of the opinions of others? This is exactly what happened to the Samaritan woman and what happened to me.

People in my life had convinced me that I was incapable, inept, and unsuitable. I did not compare GOD's word to man's word so I decided that man was right about me. I had no biblical comparison so I believed man. But JESUS refused to give up on me just like HE refused to give up on the Samaritan woman. HE wanted to bless me and have a relationship with me but I had to give the power back to GOD by meditating on HIS word. I found three key phrases that allowed me to erase man's words: 1) GOD is with me; 2) GOD is for me; and 3) GOD is in me. By relying on these three phrases, I was able to overwrite the human words with GOD's words which deepened my relationship with CHRIST.

GOD is for me (Romans 8:31, New International Version):

MAN'S WORDS:

The Samaritan woman learned that GOD is for her in verse 10. In verse 10, JESUS says: "If you knew the gift of GOD and who it is that asks you for a drink, you would have asked him and he would have given you living water" (NIV). She meditated on these words and was eventually saved. Hallelujah! I learned that GOD is for me during college. I meditated on HIS word and I, too, was eventually saved from the doomed words spoken over my life.

I was a typical college student. I enjoyed classes. I had a good group of girlfriends. I enjoyed an active social life. Life was great until the end of my Sophomore year when I met with my advisor to discuss career goals. I told this advisor about my plans for after graduation. Without hesitation, the advisor shot back, "You will never be a Clinical Psychologist. Your grades aren't good enough. Your best bet is to be a social worker." I was shocked. I sank into the chair in her office in disbelief. I had surrounded myself with encouragers. This was my first exposure to a discourager. She had no regard for me, no regard for my dreams, and no idea that I was a child of GOD. She simply saw me as a number and that number did not impress her. That's when I recalled Romans 8:31.

GOD's WORDS:

To replace this woman's words, I began to recite Romans 8:31. My Spirit rejected this woman's picture of my future because I knew that I was *"more than a conqueror" (Romans 8:37)*. What she said had little value because she was not my Creator. I knew that all things would work together for good because I loved the LORD (Romans 8:28).

Very quickly, the image came to mind of the only psychology professor I knew. I immediately went to his office and told him about the meeting with the advisor. His first question to me was, "Who are you?" I naively thought that since I knew him, he knew me. Obviously, in a class of more than 100 students, I had not stood out to him. After formally introducing myself, he asked me to repeat my story while he listened patiently. The professor recognized the GOD in me. GOD's grace and mercy were revealed in the kindness of this stranger.

GOD's unmerited favor compelled this professor to help me. Within minutes, he was introducing me to other faculty members who would serve as mentors for the rest of my college career. Some might call this moment fate, luck, or chance. This was GOD showing up for me just like HE did for the Samaritan woman at the well. By knowing GOD's Word, the opposition of man was replaced by GOD's provision.

> BY KNOWING GOD'S WORD, THE OPPOSITION OF MAN WAS REPLACED BY GOD'S PROVISION.

GOD is in me (1John 4:4-6)

MAN'S WORDS:

The Samaritan woman learned that GOD is in her when JESUS says: *"....whoever drinks the water I give them will never thirst. Indeed, the water I give them will become in them a spring of water welling up to eternal life" 1John 4:14.* The words of man aren't designed to build you up; they're really designed to tear you down. I met a disqualifying person with destructive words at my first job. I meditated on the words in 1 John 4:4-6 to change these unkind words into useable and useful words.

After graduation, I took a job out of state and away from family. The townspeople were cold and unfriendly. I ignored these regional differences because I was excited to work with my boss and to work at a very prestigious job. My future boss was a celebrated professional with an impressive track record of success. I expected to learn great things from him. I just knew that my career would be put in high gear after working at this job. He was wise. He was intelligent. He was accomplished. And I quickly learned that he hated me.

It's still unclear what I did or didn't do to make him hate me so. I don't ever remember saying something mean about him, his family, or his work. I don't remember being disrespectful or degrading. I had only high praise for him and his work. I truly felt privileged to work with him. Yet, he did not like me at all.

At first, it wasn't overly obvious to me that I wasn't liked. I assumed that the uncomfortable meetings were just growing pains. I knew I needed to learn his system and I accepted being the "low man on the totem pole." I figured that we would grow to love and respect each other. After all, I had worked with a bunch of bosses---all with very different personalities---and we eventually found our way to friendship. I was very confident that the same would happen with my new boss. I was very wrong!

His dislike for me grew stronger and stronger each day. At first, he did not like my work. Then the feedback got very personal. He told me that I was a poorly trained worker and a poor quality person! Our meetings were tense. He set unrealistic goals for me and when I couldn't reach them, I felt like a failure. I cried every day on my way to work. The other employees started to steer clear of me so I often felt isolated and alone on the job. I spent my evenings dreading work the next day. In a short span of time, I forgot about the words found in 1John 4. I no longer believed that GOD was in me. I started to see myself as he did----worthless, incompetent, and a failure. I felt trapped and had accepted my life and this new view of me.

GOD's Words:

Luckily GOD does not abandon HIS words. GOD began to draw me to HIMSELF and I was eventually able to replace the disqualifying words of man with the life affirming words of CHRIST. By reciting 1John 4:4, I learned that the JESUS in me was drawn back to the Creator and though this hardship I was saved.

I was attending church irregularly because my work experience had beat me down. I mostly wanted to stay in bed with the covers pulled over my head. One Sunday, an acquaintance asked me to come listen to his grandmother preach at a different church in a neighboring town. The new church was small but quaint. In a former life, the church building had been a Jewish synagogue. The interior was beautifully decorated with stained glass windows and gold fixtures. The congregation was warm and inviting. I don't think I've ever been hugged so much in my life. I was accepted upon arrival.

Kimberly Morris

My friend's grandmother was a beautiful woman of GOD. She was a very tall, big-boned woman with a full head of natural gray hair that looked white against her mocha skin. Her smile was infectious. Her laugh was contagious. And her sermon was Heaven sent. She preached on the 365 "fear nots" in the bible. I was intrigued by the woman and the church. I went back to that church again and again. Each sermon reminded me of GOD's words about me and about the life GOD had for me. I loved this church. I couldn't wait for Wednesday night mid-week service and Sunday service.

One Sunday, I was asked to join the church. I initially declined the offer, just like the Samaritan woman had declined JESUS' offer (John 4:9). Like her, I didn't feel worthy of their open arms. After all, I had just spent time with a boss who hated me. How could these people see value and worth in me?

But JESUS continued to draw my spirit to HIMSELF. He sent Father James Buzzelli into my life. I used every logical reason why this prayerful group had made the wrong choice just like the Samaritan woman did. But JESUS kept telling me, just as HE told her, that salvation was mine. Hallelujah!

I began to meditate on 1John 4:4 and my spirit began to doubt the accuracy of the picture of me painted by my boss. I knew the GOD in me was greater than anyone in this world (1John 4:4). If my GOD was in me, loving me, then I wanted to know who HE said I was. So, every day, I would ask HIM and

Meet me at the Well

through HIS word, I learned that my boss' opinion of me was so wrong. I'm a masterpiece (Ephesians 2:10, New Living Translation). Masterpieces are unique and exquisite. They transcend time. GOD's picture of me did not match my boss' picture of me at all. And the GOD in me recognized GOD's picture of me. I stopped crying and I got busy. I started looking for a new job with a new boss. At the end, I had a new job with a new boss whom I love to this day. My new boss, Dr. Sandy Kornblith, became a mentor who continues to sow into my life today. His kindness has blessed my life and the life of my children. I feel honored to call him friend. This was made

possible because the GOD in me refused to let the words of man destroy HIS image.

GOD is with me (Psalm 118:6, NLT)

MAN'S WORDS:

The words of man can be discouraging. The Samaritan woman learned about discouragement in verse 16-17. JESUS asks her about her husband and she said that she has no husband. Failed relationships can be very discouraging. My relationship with GOD deepened when I realized that GOD is with me. He is my helper (Psalm 118:7, NIV). I can trust HIM (Psalm 118:8). Knowing these facts about JESUS allowed me to replace the negativity of man with hope and perseverance, just like the Samaritan woman at the well.

Kimberly Morris

I am a single mother of two very active girls. Extra income is welcomed for life's uncertainties. So, I began to pray for a way to make the extra money that we needed to make ends meet.

I sent my resume to a local university with hopes of getting hired. My dreams of employment were quickly dashed when the department secretary told me that the department was not receiving any new applications. I asked if I could leave my resume on file and she responded with a definite, "NO!" These words were discouraging to me.

GOD's WORDS:

I began to read and re-read Psalm 118:6. I continued to pray and seek GOD's guidance on earning extra income. I heard the LORD urging me in an entirely different direction-- volunteerism. I thought I had misheard the LORD. I needed money. Volunteering fits my value and beliefs but volunteering was not going to add to my bottom line. So I studied Psalm 118:6 and I prayed more. Again, I heard that I needed to trust GOD's direction by getting involved in local groups and organizations. So, as an act of obedience, I got involved in local groups that appealed to me. As I got involved, I discovered that I really enjoyed the time spent on local issues that mattered to the community. Fundraisers and voter registration aligned with my commitment to bettering the lives of my fellow townspeople.

One day, the President of one of the organizations announced that our small group was partnering with the local university. We were hosting a welcome reception for the new University President and Vice-President. I was very excited to meet these two influential people and learn more about the university's plan to build in the community. As the plans for the reception were coming together, one of the board members leaned over to me and said, "Bring your resume." The day arrived and I was so excited. Within a few minutes at the reception, I found myself face to face with the President and the Vice President. We exchanged brief pleasantries and I nervously mentioned that I had my resume with me. The University President smiled and graciously asked, "May I see your resume?" He scanned it quickly and noted that I was an alumna of the university. He looked shocked and said, "Why aren't you working for us?" I told him that I had tried for many years to get a job on the campus. He looked shocked and told me to contact his office on Monday. I followed through with his direction and I started working with the department the next term.

GOD's plans for me came to fruition despite the discouraging words spoken to me by the department secretary. By trusting GOD and relying on HIS power, I secured the position that was destined for me. This was made possible because I meditated on Psalm 118.

CONCLUSION
My experiences with GOD, man, and words are not unique.

When at a crossroads, we must decide who we are going to believe, GOD or man. Man may encourage or he may discourage. GOD is with us, for us, and in us. So, man can never have the final say in our lives. Always verify what is said about you by man by what is said about you by GOD. We demonstrate wisdom when we use the Bible to send and receive appreciation and affirmation. Just as with the Samaritan woman at the well, we develop a closer relationship with CHRIST when we believe JESUS and reject human statements.

Meet me at the Well

Evelyn Oglesby

Evelyn R. Oglesby is a well-rounded powerhouse in the Kingdom of God. Her sound Christian family upbringing, stability in the ways of God, and ethical business practices has helped her in rearing her four children, assisting in Pastoral duties as First Lady at Great Faith Christian Center, owning and operating Hobson's Professional Drycleaning and Laundry in Kokomo, Indiana; and mentoring aspiring entrepreneurs.

Meet me at the Well

Lady Evelyn is a dedicated woman to her passions and there is nothing she is more passionate about than her relationship with the Lord Jesus Christ. She is also known throughout the body of Christ as an anointed gospel singer and encourager of men and women everywhere.

Lady Evelyn is married to Pastor Romon Rodrick Oglesby, Sr.; and together they are bringing up their family, Calah Unique, Corinth Joy, Christian Love, and Romon Rodrick II, to love God first and keep Him as the center of their lives.

Enjoy the ministry of Lady Evelyn Oglesby.

Evelyn Oglesby

A Walk In Miracles

I've always known that God was real. It was taught to me as early as I can remember. My grandfather was a bishop in the Church of God in Christ, Inc. My dad was a pastor, and my mom, along with my dad, were prayer warriors. I've seen miracles and supernatural demonstration of what the power of God can do. God has always been a vital part of my growing up. Signs and wonders were no strange thing, or something I heard about. The testimonies were true. The people weren't actors, because I knew them personally. The situations weren't made up, because I watched life happen. But yet, there was something missing in my life.

I made the decision to make Jesus Lord of my life the first Sunday night in April 1984. Our church was in revival services with Evangelist Jessie Dickens from Oakland, California. He would often come to our church to conduct revivals. The whole church would get ready, both spiritually and naturally. We would start fasting and praying for souls to be saved, sick bodies to be healed, and for the Lord to fill His people with His

Holy Spirit. In our house, even the children fasted. Though exciting for some, all the children knew revival meant no food until lunchtime, that every night of the revival we would have to sit on the front rows, and after the preaching go to the altar to "tarry" for the Holy Ghost. That meant for us, clapping our hands really fast, saying the name of Jesus over and over, or uttering some form of praise repeatedly until the power of God fell on you, giving you a personal experience with God. Well, that night as Evangelist Dickens was preaching, it seemed as though I was hearing the message of salvation for the very first time, but I knew it wasn't. I heard it preached many times, but this time was different. I actually heard the good news. The Evangelist preached with power, clarity, and with what I later found out was revelation. When he was done preaching, Evangelist Dickens asked if anyone wanted the baptism of the Holy Ghost to come to the altar. I was ready and I wanted it so much so, that I was one of the first ones to the altar. As the Evangelist prayed, I clapped my hands as hard as I could, saying "Fill me, Lord!" over and over again. Tears formed in my eyes and began to run down my face. There was a change starting to take place on the inside of me, and I knew it! The overwhelming sense of joy that I felt in that very moment caused my feet to move and I couldn't stay in the same space I was occupying. I knew there were other people on the altar with me, but I wasn't concerned with them. My body swayed from side to side as I clapped my hands. My words changed from "Fill me, Lord" to "Thank you, Lord for filling me with the Holy Ghost." My personal space began to expand. I'm not sure how many people I moved

Evelyn Oglesby

out of my way, but the altar became my very own. God heard my prayer, and He answered me right there, that night. One minute I was dancing in the Spirit. The next minute I was not there. I had left my physical body. I don't remember seeing anyone or

> IT WAS AS IF GOD'S HAND CRADLED MY HEAD.

any objects. Everything was pure white. All I could see was white. Such a peace! Nevertheless, I could see myself lying on the floor on my back. I looked as if I was sleeping. The rest I experienced at that very moment was like nothing I had ever experienced before. It was as if God's hand cradled my head. I wasn't thinking about anything. It was just a moment of overwhelming peace. I knew I was in God's presence. I had no care in the world. Nothing mattered at all. This world, nor anything in it was of any relevance. Only God! All of a sudden, I was disturbed from this peace. I opened my eyes, and I was back in my physical body. I really was lying on the floor near a small table in a corner at the front of the church, where the deacons would sit. Several ladies were helping me up off of the floor. My legs were so weak. I couldn't stand on my own, so they sat me down on the front pew. I was trying to figure out how and when did I get on the floor. All I knew was I had a spiritual encounter in God's holy presence while everyone else was around. I knew my sins had been forgiven; I had been washed clean, and that God's Holy Spirit now occupied my very soul. I felt like nothing would or could ever harm me, and empowered to live for Jesus the rest of my days. My dad brought me a microphone and asked me,

"Daughter, what did the Lord do for you tonight?" I responded happily and said, "He filled me, He filled me!" Others that came to the altar had the same testimony, but it felt as if I was the only one in that church. I left from there rejoicing and praising God. I was 11 years old, to be 12 the very next month. God had touched my life that night, so that I'd be able to get through tough moments in my adult life.

THE HOLY SPIRIT IN ACTION

I went on to live for Jesus through high school and college. I experienced challenges as other teenagers do, but having God's spirit was my saving grace in many situations. I met a young boy who on the first day of my 10th grade year in high school, approached me just before the start of Chemistry class and said, "God told mse you are going to be my wife." I looked up as to see where this, what I thought was foolish, voice was coming from. I immediately responded to him, "Satan, the Lord rebukes you!" I don't remember any other conversation, but I do remember the bell ringing and class had begun. The next day I noticed that particular boy was not in class. He had been transferred to another class. As time went on we'd see each other from time to time, because our families traveled in similar circles. We did later become friends, and after going to college, began to date. I hated knowing that I had spoken such harsh words to him back in 10th grade, but he forgave me and became the love of my life. On July 16, 1994, we became husband and wife.

Evelyn Oglesby

My husband and I were happy moving in the direction of God's leading. We were enjoying each other, and our two daughters, at that time. I got pregnant again and delivered my 3rd daughter four weeks early in April 2001. Three children under the age of 5 was a challenge. I was a stay-at-home mom, and thought I was managing and adjusting very well. I had my hands full, but I loved being home with my babies. I began to notice at 2 months old, Christian Love (who my oldest daughter named), was becoming lethargic and somewhat non-responsive. I told my husband and he said that it was just her, and that every child was different. It sounded logical, but I just didn't feel right inside. Well on a particular Friday morning, my oldest daughter was scheduled to have a kindergarten physical. After arriving to the doctor's office, we waited in the examining room for the doctor. When the doctor came in, he greeted my two older girls then looked into the car seat to greet Christian. He immediately called for the nurse to bring him a measuring tape. I thought it strange, because Christian didn't have an appointment. He measured her head, and proceeded to examine my oldest girl. Before we left the office that day, the doctor said, "If anything changes with Christian over the weekend, call me. And I want to see her Monday." I looked at him, knowing that he was trying to tell me something without saying it. I replied, "I sure will." I told my husband what happened at the doctor's office. We both tried not to be alarmed, but watched Christian very closely over the next couple of days. Sunday, we went to church like we did every week. Different ones commented on how Christian was getting fat. That wasn't abnormal for a

Meet me at the Well

2-month-old. Still I knew in my heart something wasn't right with Christian. Later Sunday night I noticed that Christian's head was extremely hot. I checked her temperature, but she didn't have a fever. She would cry out, and then stop before I could even console her. What was happening? I was so confused; however, God wouldn't let me worry or get anxious. When Monday came I got the girls dressed and we headed to the doctor's office. The doctor came in the exam room, and did the same thing as before. He immediately called for the nurse to bring a measuring tape. Christian's head had grown a whole inch in 3 days. He said, "I want to do a CT Scan right away. But first I'm going to have you go to the pharmacy to get medicine to sedate Christian, because she must be very still for the procedure." I would not ask the doctor any questions, because I did not want to hear what his answers might be. When I left the doctor's office, not only did I go to the pharmacy, but I also took this opportunity to go by my Pastor's house, along with others, for prayer. Not sure what news I would later get, but I needed the prayers of the righteous to intercede for my baby and for the comforting power of the Holy Spirit. By the time I made it back to the doctor's office for the CT Scan, the word had spread to other members of our church that our family needed them, and they began to pour into the waiting room at the doctor's office. God's spirit was with us when we received the results that our 2-month-old had hydrocephalus; which was fluid forming on the right side of her brain. It was causing a lot of pressure and needed to be removed right away. The doctor explained to us that Christian would undergo surgery at the children's hospital one hour

Evelyn Oglesby

away involving a ventricular shunt being placed inside her head to drain the fluid, and relieve the pressure. What news! My husband and I were devastated, and everyone knew it. One of the elders from our church asked everyone with us to join hands as he lead us in prayer for peace and healing. Even though the moment was full of questions and anguish, God's hand cradled us and carried us all the way to the hospital where Christian would have surgery. A dear friend from the church drove us to the hospital, and played a powerful prayer CD by Bishop Charles H. Mason, who was the founder of the Church of God in Christ, Inc. The presence of the Holy Spirit became that comforter mentioned in St. John 14:26, 27: *"But the Comforter, which is the Holy Ghost, whom the Father will send in my name, he shall teach you all things, and bring all things to your remembrance, whatsoever I have said unto you. Peace, I leave with you, my peace I give unto you: not as the world giveth, give I unto you. Let not your heart be troubled, neither let it be afraid."* (King James Version) I received the power of peace through the Holy Spirit, because I within myself was powerless for my baby girl. I remember as I sat in the room at the children's hospital with Christian's godmother, a little old lady about 5 feet tall appeared in the doorway, with silver hair,

> EVEN THOUGH THE MOMENT WAS FULL OF QUESTIONS AND ANGUISH, GOD'S HAND CRADLED US AND CARRIED US ALL THE WAY TO THE HOSPITAL WHERE CHRISTIAN WOULD HAVE SURGERY.

wearing a purple and white striped shirt, and purple pants. I did not know her, nor had I ever seen her before. She stretched her hand towards Christian and began to say these words, "Father, I pray for this baby. Satan, take your hands off of her. Father, touch and heal her now. In Jesus' name, Amen" and walked away. I jumped up to go to her to thank her for praying, but when I looked in the hall no one was there. God had sent an angel to keep watch over us through this ordeal. What a mighty God we serve! My husband and I stood in faith for healing for our precious and helpless infant. The surgery was the next morning without any incidents.

As Christian grew older, my husband and I taught her to have faith in God, and how to walk in her healing. She stood in faith and continued to be in faith even at eight years old, when we learned that fluid was forming on the left side of her brain. It seemed as if we were reliving a nightmare. But again, the Holy Spirit was our comforter and peace. Having to go through another surgery was not what we would have chosen for our daughter. We just continued to trust God for His healing. Christian often said, "I am healed!" In spite of it all, the Holy Spirit empowered us to go through this storm, and come out better than when we entered the storm. Many other health challenges attacked her body but we continued to stand on the Word of God. *"The righteous person may have many troubles, but the Lord delivers him from them all." (Psalm 34:19, New International Version)* We just continued to pray and wholly lean on Jesus. My Christian Love is 16 years old today and is healed from every sickness. To God Be The

Evelyn Oglesby

Glory!

The Holy Spirit has been prevalent in my life ever since that beautiful Sunday night in April 1984. He's been a friend that walks with me through every high and low moment in my life. His presence in my life supersedes anything else I have ever experienced. I praise God for sending such a wonderful companion of himself to dwell with mankind. The Holy Spirit is always in action in my life.

Meet me at the Well

Jackie Thomas-Miller

A former public school administrator and special education teacher, Dr. Jacquelyn Thomas-Miller is currently an administrator at Purdue University. A lifelong educator, she is passionate about adding value to others. Dr. Jackie is the CEO/Co-Founder of The Alternative Research Development and Educational Center (TARDEC, LLC) in Kokomo, Indiana. One of the major focuses of TARDEC is educational consuiting. Jackie stays connected to education as an Adjunct Professor at Indiana Wesleyan University, responsible for the online instruction of those seeking Principal Licensure. An internationally certified Leadership Development Speaker and Trainer, Dr. Jackie is an author, certified Emotional Intelligence consultant, and John Maxwell YouthMAX Plus Facilitator. As a servant leader within her community and beyond, she shares her gifts, time, and talent on numerous Executive and Advisory Boards for state and local organizations. Seeking to be proactive in civil leadership, Dr. Jackie ran as the Democratic candidate for Howard County Auditor during the November 2016 election. Although, she was defeated by the incumbent auditor, Dr. Jackie welcomed the opportunity to connect with her community at a different level.

Dr. Jackie is married to (Ret.) Lt. Col. John T. Miller, and the proud mother of four adult children, Serenthia, Imhotep, Osiris, and Ramses and doting grandmother of two talented granddaughters, Olivia and Zenobia. She cherishes family time and being an active member of Alpha Mu Omega Chapter, Alpha Kappa Alpha Sorority, Inc. in Indianapolis, IN.

Jackie Thomas-Miller

Believing

"May the God of hope fill you with all joy and peace in believing, so that by the power of the Holy Spirit you may abound in hope." Romans 15:13 (King James Version)

This chapter has caused me to unveil scars that I had so strategically learned to cover and now openly expose my vulnerability. It is important that I share this story of truth focused on my early years with the hopes of touching the lives of other young ladies who have experienced similar circumstances in their turbulent journey in life. I believe that God had a plan for my life. Although my path was tainted with traumatic experiences, it is these same experiences that ultimately molded me into the woman that I am today. I am now a mature woman who believes in the power of prayer and persistence and seeks to provide solace to others by telling my story.

Meet me at the Well

MY PLACE OF REFUGE

"Be sober, be vigilant; because your adversary the devil, as a roaring lion, walketh about, seeking whom he may devour." 1 Peter 5:8

My childhood and adolescence were filled with disappointment, shame, and ridicule. The emotional pain I felt superseded the physical pain and abuse. Domestic violence in the home abounded. To hide the pain and fear, I would sit and dream….dream of having a loving family… dream of becoming a successful woman in business…dream of going to college….dreaming always of a better life. I was in constant prayer not quite understanding why God would take me through such painful events time and time again. When little girls were playing with make-believe friends, I was always pretending that I lived in a loving home. Not to take away from my mother's love for her children, however, during my primary and preteen years, I didn't feel my mother's arms of protection. It was later that I realized that it was a result of her being broken and torn. My two brothers and I were so fortunate to have a great circle of extended family members and friends who embraced us with kindness. For this, I am forever grateful.

School became my place of refuge. It was in school that I could escape into another world. A world of acceptance and laughter that overshadowed my secret world at home. I was so determined to do my best at all times. My teachers became the inspirational role models that I needed. There were several teachers who took the time to expose me to cultural events and activities that I would have never been exposed to. Year after year, I proudly wore the title of teacher's pet. It was in school that I sought the love and approval that I had bottled up in my heart. I was a student who worked hard, compensated, and pushed myself to overcome academic obstacles so that I could come out shining. Report cards were my medals of honor. It was also in school that my love for perfumes took root. I could never get enough of smelling the wonderful scents of my female teachers as they walked by my desk. I found myself purposely calling them over to answer meaningless questions just to get another whiff. However, the solace I found in school was constantly diminished by the fear that existed behind the doors of my home.

A Child's Determination

"And it came to pass, when the Philistine arose, and came and drew nigh to meet David, that David hasted, and ran toward the army to meet the Philistine." 1 Samuel 17:48

Although my family had little money, I refused to let it get me down. Having a strong work ethic and never settling for status quo were two specific traits that I inherited from my father. I was always seeking to improve my abilities. I taught myself how to sew and to type at an early age. I remember sewing clothes for my dolls by hand from scraps of fabric and making outfits for my paper dolls. When I wasn't doing that I was sitting at the kitchen table looking at the wall clock with the will of determination to increase my typing speed. Yes, at the age of 11, I had asked for a portable typewriter for Christmas and a Singer sewing machine the next Christmas. Since our Christmas list was limited to one prime gift, my mindset was on obtaining a gift that would help me grow. Even at a young age, I was guided to believe that these skills would benefit me well later in life. I knew that the only things that I had any control of in my life were my gifts and talents.

> I KNEW THAT THE ONLY THINGS THAT I HAD ANY CONTROL OF IN MY LIFE WERE MY GIFTS AND TALENTS.

HOPELESSNESS

"My God, my God, why hast thou forsaken me? Why art thou so far from helping me, and from the words of my roaring?" Psalms 22:1

As I entered into adolescence, I leaned on my friends for guidance in the area of teenage sex and pregnancy. I was also in the state of confusion as to why grown men had for years sought to violate the innocence and vulnerability of a broken child. As I continued to look for love in all the wrong places, I was naïve in thinking that the young man I was fond of cared about the consequences of unprotected sex as much as I did. My self-esteem and self-worth was so low that it didn't matter that he was also seeing other girls while seeing me. As a result, I became pregnant soon after the start of my junior year of high school. In the late 1970's, teenage pregnancies were shunned upon by the public school system. Young mothers either dropped out of school or in effort to remain in school, covered up their pregnancies. On top of it, the father of my unborn child's parents were adamant that I have an abortion stating that without it, their son nor I would have a successful future. They were not taking into consideration that I was three months pregnant by the time they found out. It was the most notable time in my life in which my mother put her foot down and absolutely opposed it. She expressed that she would do whatever she needed to help me complete school. I proceeded to go into a hollow hole of depression. My mother encouraged me to keep my head held high. However, completing that task proved to become beyond difficult. During my private times, I remember crying that now my dreams of ever having a bright future were crushed. My hope for a bright future was gone.

ONE WOMAN'S VISION

"For I was hungry and you gave me something to eat, I was thirsty and you gave me something to drink, I was a stranger and you invited me in." Matthew 25:35

Having heard of a place called Florence Crittenton (Toledo, OH), which was designed specifically for teenage unwed mothers to continue their education, I transferred there in the early spring of my junior year in high school. I still recall sitting outside the director's office, the door opening and seeing my mother wiping tears from her eyes as the director came to me and stated that I had been admitted to attend school and would be living there also as a resident. Although there were a large number of teenage girls attending the school, there were only two other local girls living in residence as the other six beds were of girls from other surrounding cities and/or states. Florence Crittenton also provided a daycare for the mothers to continue their schooling so that they didn't have that worry, when the baby was born.

> I LEFT THE HOSPITAL WITH A SENSE OF RENEWAL. I WAS STRONGER AND SET ON BECOMING THE ADULT I KNEW I COULD BE.

Unbeknown to me, it was at Florence Crittenton that my self-esteem began to flourish. The wounds of defeat and discouragement were starting to heal. I started to lift my head again and smile. I enjoyed going to class and learning new things, particularly the courses on childbirth and prenatal care. I still cherish the time spent talking with the director who also taught me how to knit an afghan. I still have that afghan to this day and it has been used by all of my four children and two granddaughters. Although, at the time, I didn't know just how exactly I was going to make life better for myself and my unborn child, I truly believed that I could make it somehow and knew that it had to begin with me! Four months later,

I gave birth to a healthy and beautiful daughter. I left the hospital with a sense of renewal. I was stronger and set on becoming the adult I knew I could be. It was as though my life was beginning to evolve in a different direction. I was now a mother and I wanted to fulfill that role to the best of my ability. Leaning on a quote by John Maxwell, he stated, "You begin to make a better life by making better decisions."

FORGIVENESS

"Brethren, I count not myself to have apprehended: but this one thing I do, forgetting those things which are behind, and reaching forth unto those things which are before, I press toward the mark for the prize of the high calling of God in Christ Jesus." Philippians 3:13-14

Throughout the remainder of my senior year in high school and college years, I always believed that there were better possibilities available for me and my daughter! I pursued greatness in myself as a college student who would bring her child to evening classes, when necessary. All honor goes to my professors at Jackson State University who expected only the best from me and wouldn't allow any less. It was in college that I came to realize that the scars of my past had continuously caused me to sabotage any intimate relationship that came my way. I came to this profound understanding through my constant teachings of the word of God that it wasn't until I began to forgive, that I was able to unleash the pent-up anger that I had kept concealed for so many years and find peace and true love. It wasn't until I began to forgive that I was able to stop sabotaging my relationships with others and denying myself the true life that God had laid out for me. It wasn't until I began to forgive that I was able to openly embrace my parents with the love that I always had for them as their daughter. The anger that I had buried deep within had started to unleash its ugly head. Through constant prayer and trust in the Lord, I was successfully able to put a controllable lid on it and experience the true peace within that I had so desperately needed. Admittedly, there have been brief moments in time, when the devil has tried to loosen my grip on the lid. This is where I must stay at war with the devil in keeping my salvation and trust in God intact. I no longer blame my parents for my painful childhood for I now know their stories. Motivational speaker, Les Brown said it best, "Forgive anyone who has caused you pain or harm. Keep in mind that forgiving is not for others. It is for you. Forgiving is not forgetting. It is remembering without anger. It frees up your power, heals your body, mind and spirit. Forgiveness opens up a pathway to a new place of peace where you can persist despite what has happened to you."

TIME TO SOAR

"He has shown you, O mortal, what is good. And what does the LORD require of you? To act justly and to love mercy and to walk humbly with your God." Micah 6:8

Although my journey continues to be one that experiences a

Jackie Thomas-Miller

few detours and bumps in the road, I know without a doubt that my life has been divinely guided through Grace. My dark past prepared me for my life's work. I do have a purpose! I am unable to humanly explain why the Lord allowed such pain to dwell in my young life, but I can declare that it is because of that pain I now glow from the Glory and Grace of God. The enemy still lurks in corners shouting words of discernment, in attempts to distract me. However, I am very intentional about being an active community servant and educational leader who is passionate about addressing the pressing issues surrounding our most vulnerable girls and families. It is with hope that this testimony provides a source of comfort and healing.

I am forever grateful to Florence Crittenton, now known as The National Crittenton Foundation, along with my elementary teachers and extended family members for lifting me back up from a lost and broken spirit! For it was as a result having lived in a home for unwed mothers that my belief in self began to soar! As I choose the life of an eagle, I am often asked when I will relax and slow down. Those who ask just don't understand the depth of my life's purpose and the level of my commitment to what I do. It is my unwavering faith that provides me with an overflow of inner peace and power to share the gifts that God has blessed me with. I sing praises of triumph and victory as the loving wife of a Christian man, (Ret) Lt. Col. John T. Miller; proud mother of four adult children, Serenthia, Imhotep, Osiris, and Ramses; doting grandmother of two talented little girls, Olivia and Zenobia; and most importantly a loving daughter of Carolyn and Sidney Thomas and caring sister to Derrick Sr. and Sidney, Jr. I know that the legacy that I desire to leave will not be defined by the multiple scholarly degrees that I possess or positions of power that I have acquired. It is defined by my genuine acts to serve all mankind as I seek to add value to the lives of those within my area of influence.

I'll close by sharing this conversation. In 2007, while driving home from an event with my eldest teenage son, Imhotep, I curiously asked, "How would you describe your mom in one word?" Without hesitation, he instinctively replied, "Strong." If only he knew just how much that meant to me…

Author Information:

Pastor Sharon Reed
www.esthersplaceboutique.com
sarc332@gmail.com
(765) 419-4140

Essie Foster
cheffortheday.essie@yahoo.com

Danelle Cottle
Fullofgrace507@gmail.com

Lewis & DeElla Hall
Lewisjhall@aol.com   (765) 438-9479
Kingdomtravel03@gmail.com   (765) 271-9487

Raenay Judeika
Total Rethink Pedi Mani Body Care & Gifts
4031 S. Webster
Kokomo, IN 46902
ispa4dreams@comcast.net
www.facebook.com/TotalRethink
www.facebook.com/Raenay.Judeika

Karon Lancaster
karonlancaster@gmail.com

Margie Lea
Margielea1985@yahoo.com

Carolyn R Loftis
Lofttax@msn.com
(765) 457-1424

Dr. Kimberly Morris
Inspiredlife4you@gmail.com
www.facebook.com/InspirationforLife
(765) 461-4099

Evelyn Oglesby
ladyeoglesby@gmail.com
(765) 205-1168

Dr. Jacquelyn Thomas-Miller
CEO/Co-Founder, TARDEC, LLC
700 E. Firmin Street, Suite 253
Kokomo, IN 46902

Notes:

Meet me at the Well

Notes:

Treasures fit for a Queen!

Esther's Place Boutique
414 W Taylor Street
Kokomo, IN
765-419-4140

Open Fridays 10-3 or Call for Appointment

www.esthersplaceboutique.com

Celebrating our 10th year!

COUPON
GOOD FOR $10 OFF
$50 PURCHASE

... treasures fit for a Queen!

414 W Taylor Street
Kokomo, Indiana
www.esthersplaceboutique.com

Open Fridays 10-3
Call for an appointment
765-419-4140
Good for $10 off $50 purchase!

Meet me at the Well

AUTHENTIC IDENTITY COACHING PRESENTS

MY STORY GOD'S GLORY • A PEACE OF ME • HIDDEN IDENTITY • A GLIMPSE OF GLORY

AIC PUBLISHED BOOKS   AIC PUBLISHED BOOKS

**ARE YOU READY TO BECOME AN AUTHOR?
BECOME AN AUTHOR IN AIC'S NEXT BOOK COLLABORATION. YOU WILL RECEIVE...**

BOOKS | TRAINING
ACCOUNTABILITY | PROFESSIONAL HEADSHOT
PUBLISHED AUTHOR STATUS | SOCIAL MEDIA ADVERTISEMENT
PROFESSIONAL BOOK LAUNCH & SIGNING AND MORE...

ASK US HOW!
WWW.AUTHENTICINSTITUTE.COM

THREE-DAY INTENSIVE
5D COACHING CERTIFICATION

TRAINING TO BECOME A 5D AUTHENTICALLY ME CERTIFIED COACH WILL BE CONDUCTED USING BOTH LIVE AND WEBINAR FORMATS. THE TRAINING AREAS WILL INCLUDE:

HUMAN BEHAVIOR CONSULTANT CERTIFICATION
SUMMARY OF COACHING PROFESSION
5D SEMINAR TRAINING
FACILITATION/PRESENTER TRAINING

COACH TIMEKO WHITAKER
FOUNDER/CEO

FOR MORE INFO VISIT: AUTHENTICINSTITUTE.COM